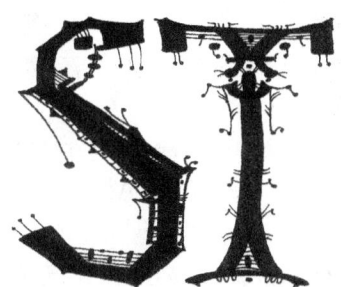

< Also by Sotère Torregian >

The Age of Gold (Redux): Poems 1967-1975,
Rêve à Deux, Vacaville, 2014

On the Planet without Visa: Selected Poetry and Other Writings,
AD 1960-2012, Coffee House Press, Minneapolis, 2012

Envoy, Punch Press, Buffalo, 2010

"I Must Go" (She Said) "Because My Pizza's Cold": Selected Works,
1957-1999, Skanky Possum, Austin, 2002

Always for the First Time, Kolourmeim Press / Co-Published by
Pantograph Press, Oakland / Berkeley, 1999

The Young Englishwoman, Privately published by Friends of
the Poet, Palo Alto, 1989

Amtrak trek: Being Poems And Prose Written Cross-Country From
California To New York, Telephone Books, New York, 1979

The Age of Gold (Poems 1968-1970), Kulchur Foundation,
New York, 1976

The Wounded Mattress, Oyez, Berkeley, 1970

The Golden Palomino Bites The Clock, Angel Hair, New York, 1967

< Also from *Rêve à Deux* >

Marie Wilson & Nanos Valaoritis *Land of Diamond,* 2015
Sotère Torregian *The Age of Gold (Redux),* 2014
Will Alexander *The Brimstone Boat – For Philip Lamantia,* 2012
Schlechter Duvall *The Adventures of Desirée,* 2009

Surreal Adventurer

SOTÈRE TORREGIAN
Surreal Adventurer

WITH TWELVE INK DRAWINGS BY
BRIAN LUCAS

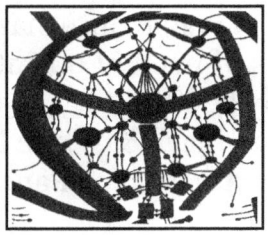

Rêve à Deux

Oakland - Stockton - Vacaville

Copyright © 2015 by Sotère Torregian

The cover design is by Thom Burns.

Cover Image, "A Woman I Met in Trafalgar Square June 25th 1936," collage, calligraphy, watercolor & ink, c. 1998; page 8: *"Poéme-objet, de 1971, pour < l'Age d 'or>"*, collage, 1971-97; page 167: *"Salut à le Van Gogh de notre temps"*, collage, watercolor & ink, 2011 © by Sotère Torregian. Back cover photo of Sotère © by Roulette Smith. All illustrations appearing on the following pages: Pages i, 2, 16, 32, 44, 56, 70, 82, 98, 112, 126, 138 & 152 © by Brian Lucas.

Rêve à Deux

Rêve à Deux was founded in 2009, and is edited by Richard Waara. Additional paperback copies of this book, and other *Rêve à Deux* titles, are available on Amazon.com or Lulu.com. Hardback editions of most of our titles are available exclusively at: http://www.lulu.com
This individual title has Black & White Paperback & Hardback Editions along with a Color Paperback Edition.

ISBN 978-0-578-16150-1 (Black & White Paperback Edition);
ISBN 978-0-578-16151-8 (Color Paperback Edition)

BLACK & WHITE PAPERBACK EDITION

Printed in the United States of America

CONTENTS

Ink Marker Drawing #1 by Brian Lucas: *"the swirled chambered nautilus journeys"* 2

" *Poéme-objet, de 1971, pour 'l'A ge d'or'* " by Sotère Torregian 8

The Surrealist Adventurer of Stockton, California by Dale Smith 9

A N(otA) B (ene) 15

Ink Marker Drawing #2 by Brian Lucas: *"out of the tableau"* 16

For Chitrakar, Poet & Painter of the Punjab 17

A Woman I Met in Trafalgar Square June 25th 1936 18

Amtrak Update — For Ray Burns 20

Laura 22

Passeggiata 24

Tableau for Tarun Bedi & for Kabir Bedi 26

Photo: *Paola Barbieri by Tarun Bedi* 28

On Paola's Birthday 29

Ink Marker Drawing #3 by Brian Lucas: *"in Omar Khayyám's mobile garden"* 32

L' Inconnu Arshile Gorky 33

For Arshile Gorky, the Lost Newark Airport Murals 35

Arshile Gorky —"Study for *Agony*" 37

The Young Arshile Gorky Astride his White Stallion Overlooking the Ancient Site of *Sourp Khatcha* 39

"Child of an Idumean Night" by Arshile Gorky 41

Ink Marker Drawing #4 by Brian Lucas: *"your spectre on the shores"* 44

The View From Occupied Alcatraz 45

ENTRECHAT: *Homage to Tehlirian!* 48

For the French National Assembly and Its Resolution Inditing the Turkish Nation for Its Massacre of the Armenians in 1915 50

Ink Marker Drawing #5 by Brian Lucas: *"the web of gossamer"* 56

As I Set My Pen to Paper Today (Our Dialogue Continues) 57

For Antoinette In Autun, France 59

In the Silence (After Your Voice) 62

The Poet Speaks Through the Painter's *Voice of Fire* 63

Rue de l'Abbé-de-l'Épée (For One Who Resides There) 66

Ink Marker Drawing #6 by Brian Lucas: *"With the recollection of Memory"* 70

For Queen Noor of Jordan 71

Ink Marker Drawing #7 by Brian Lucas: *"the telegraphy of slugs"* 82

For Marissa Mayer at Google 83

Temptation of the October Twilight 84

"Market Correction" 86

The Poet Is Asleep 87

Serenata 88

Horse Dregs On the Road 89

I Leave The Front Lights On At Night 90

Hommage à Cartier-Bresson 91

MM Reclining, Reading James Joyce's *Ulysses* 94

A Faded Pressed Rose Fell From the Pages 95

On a Leafy Tree-Branch at the Great Wall 96

    Ink Marker Drawing #8 by Brian Lucas: *"'optimum equilibrium'"* 98

D-Day Notes 99

At Oduvai Gorge And the "Beginnings" With "Lucy", The First (Female) Human Being 101

Ishi the Last Yahi 105

From a Letter to Donald & Luisa Stewart in Rome 108

    Ink Marker Drawing #9 by Brian Lucas: *"'were I a swan'"* 112

The House Where Karl Marx Lived (Soho, London) 113

The Price of Gold (Again) On the Market Today at $754.10 120

The Words "Handle With Care" *(apparaître tout d' un coup)* 122

L'Origine du monde 124

    Ink Marker Drawing #10 by Brian Lucas: *"in the streets of Teheran"* 126

Envoy 127

A Moment in Teheran 129

Song for Henry Winston (1911-1986) 131

The Dust of the Pharaohs Flies in the Air 133

To the Baghdad School of the Arts 134

The Bridge Across the Nile ("The Arab Spring") 136

    Ink Marker Drawing #11 by Brian Lucas: *"Total assault!"* 138

Manifesto *AU CONTRAIRE!*: On the Occasion of the Whitney Biennial 2014 139

In This Resurgence: On Reading *"Collected Poems, Joseph Ceravolo"* 146

Actuelles of Dr. Pangloss, or An Omphalic Note for *"Terre de diamant"* 148

    Ink Marker Drawing #12 by Brian Lucas: *"the 'Nomo' of the cosmos"* 152

Témoignage à Senghor 153

    Poéme-objet: "Salut à le Van Gogh de notre temps" by Sotére Torregian 167

    Drawing by My Grand-Daughter, Maya 169

... et le voyageur égaré tenait message d l'étoile
("... when a lost traveler could receive directions
 from a star")
 —Léopold Sédar Senghor, *'Élégie pour
 Aynina Fall', Nocturnes*

          *   *   *

... D'un fer pesant d'un fer ardent
Je repasse les plis du vent
 ("... As a heavy iron a burning iron
 I press the folds of the wind")
 —Paul Éluard, *Ailleurs, ici, partout*
 ("Here, There and Everywhere")

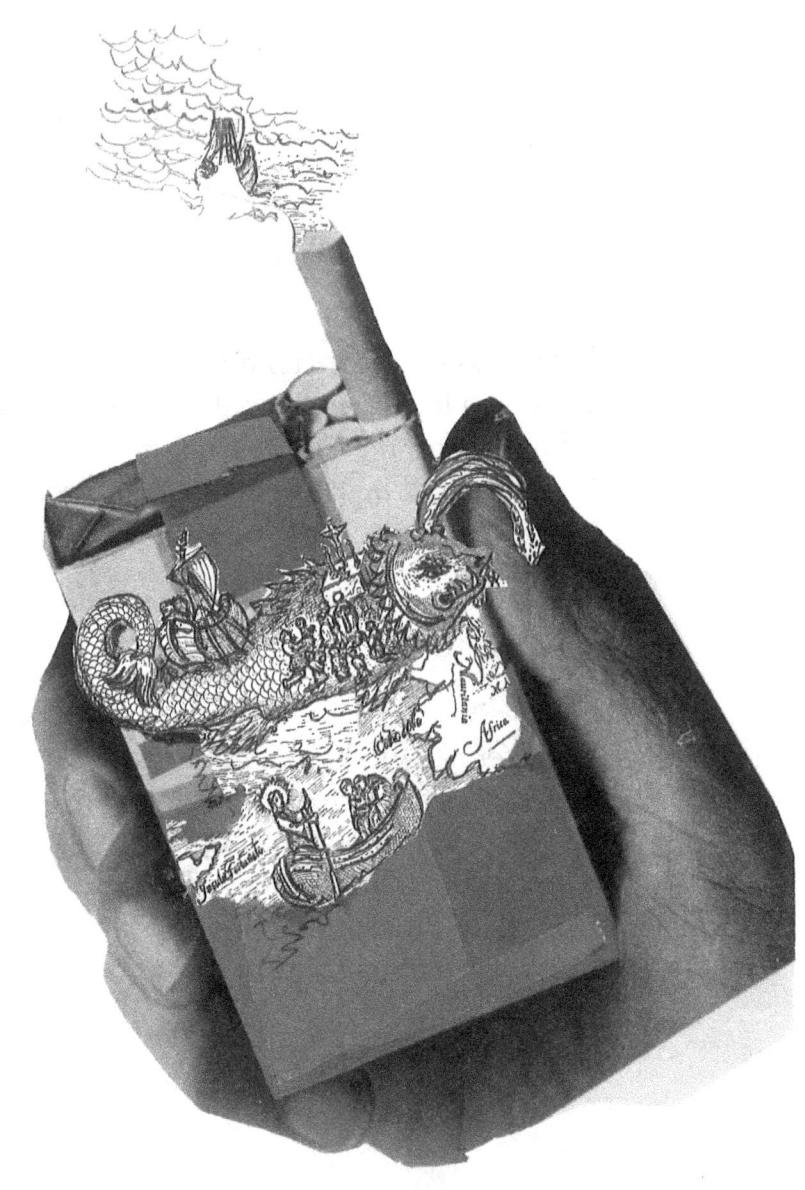

"... que si realmente el cielo es la casa de los ángeles ..." ❧
poème-objet, de 1971, pour l'Âge d'or.

— Sotère Torregian,
1971(—— 1997)

The Surrealist Adventurer of Stockton, California

Sotère Torregian, a self-identified French surrealist, perhaps the only such macédoine extant in North America today, grew up in "No Man's Land with lots of machine gun bullets flying all over the place," a place known also as Newark, New Jersey, where he was born in 1941. He lived in a multilingual home where he learned French, Italian, Greek, and Arabic, among other languages. Identifying at an early age with the Africanized Mediterranean, he learned English with difficulty. He received instruction in handwriting and manners at St. Anne's School in Newark, where he was expelled for kicking a nun.

Over the years of his youth he invented himself as a poet, attending readings at New York's Café Le Metro with Paul Blackburn, Joseph Ceravolo, and David Shapiro and publishing his first poems with *Art and Literature* (Isere, France), *Paris Review*, and Ted Berrigan's magazine *"C."* He left the East Coast for California in the late 1960s and taught in the nascent African-American Studies program at Stanford. Since then he has published over a dozen books of poetry, including *The Golden Palomino Bites the Clock* (Angel Hair, 1967), *The Age of Gold* (Kulchur, 1976), and the one I published with Hoa Nguyen: *"I Must Go" (She Said) "Because My Pizza's Cold"* (Skanky Possum, 2002). Punch Press recently published his latest collection, *Envoy*. [Since the writing of this text, in 2012 Coffee House Press published Sotère's *On the Planet without Visa: Selected Poetry and Other Writings, AD 1960-2012*; more recently, in 2014, an expanded edition of *The Age of Gold*, retitled *The Age of Gold (Redux): Poems 1967-1975*, was issued by the same publisher of the book now in your hands. *Editor's note*.]

His father, a Cuban boxer, left the family when Torregian was twelve, but his rich family heritage helped the boy identify with intersecting cultural influences from an early age. "My grandmother," he said in a recent conversation, "told stories about playing near the acropolis in the Plain of Enna in Sicily." The first story he remembers tells of a girl abducted by the devil in a town next to where his grandmother had lived. "It turns out to be the story of Persephoné," he said, "and of how she disobeyed her mother and went to pick flowers. Out of the earth the devil appeared and abducted her. So this is the story I was told until I was five. That was the intro to my ancestors' sense of poetry." This sense of poetry as the integrated and still-living myths of a people informed Torregian's poetic affinities—affinities cooked up in the ethnically diverse and often dangerous Newark neighborhoods of his youth.

While attending public schools, Torregian experienced his first taste of racism and the uncomfortable disassociation this can cause. White kids often attacked him because of his mixed African ancestry, while blacks, confused by his identification with Mediterranean cultural traditions, targeted him for trying to pass as white. He took refuge in the library to escape these displays of ethnic hostility. Compelled by his alienation from North American racial roles and performative expectations, he pursued through careful study the traditions and stories bestowed on him at home. But despite his studious nature, he "failed" at poetry, so he says, "for not writing in iambic pentameter. Like Rimbaud before me, my teachers claimed I was a dunce."

Perhaps an astrological accident in the house of Cancer preserved Torregian for the muses, despite his teachers' claim of early poetic failure. Sharing a birthday with one of the great poets of the Négritude movement—Aimé Césaire—Torregian early on identified with the Martinique native. Through such associations, Torregian imagines an interpenetrating world of forms, where personal identification registers across ethnic and racial lines to correspond more intriguingly with dispositions of the soul. His identification with the French surrealist poets also led him toward a path where personal vision, intellectual pursuit, and international movements of art crossed personal boundaries to create a broad and influential current of artistic activity. As this was inflected through Torregian's imagination, he was able to enter a community of fellow authors, and such imaginative, if hermetic, participation prepared him for his introduction, in the 1960s, to the New York School of poets.

In those days many poets congregated at the *Café Le Metro* coffeehouse on the Lower East Side. There, Torregian met Paul Blackburn and Ted Berrigan, who, he says, taught him more than anybody else. "Ted one day was walking with me," he recalls, " and he said, 'Sotère, you're a great poet but you have one problem: you're too serious. I love your work, but you're too serious.'" According to Torregian, "This changed everything. The French," he continued, "were talking about the pain of love. Ted said, 'You've got to get out of that. Put some laughter in your writing.' The absurd became more important."

A sense of the absurd has since permeated Torregian's writing, and it connects most closely to his understanding of French surrealism. But also, recalls Torregian, the sense of adventure in Eugène Ionesco's plays taught him to delight in the experience of the imagination. As he remembers it, Ionesco once said: "Any play that I write is an adventure, it's a kind of a hunt, the discovery of a universe that reveals itself to me at the presence of which I am the first to be astounded." This feeling of adventure keeps Torregian's ear alert to possibilities, and his poetry often moves at dazzling speed, connecting absurd but astonishingly concrete imagery that challenges a reader's expectations of the poem. Anne Waldman has called Torregian "one of our most radically original poets." She goes on to say that "his surreal lyricism, wild sense perceptions, strange imagery, and playful emotional trajectories are unique in contemporary poetry." At turns also politically motivated, socially conscious, and mysteriously delighted by the correspondences of history and geography at play in popular culture, Torregian's poetry charms for its generous, open-armed embrace of seemingly distant associations. For instance, "Come Back Africa" (1970) puts African American cultural history in conversation with the particular personal history of the poet. In part, it reads:

> ...there's magic in whatever a Black Man touches
> the railway the masses the drums of the *Metro*
> Satan's chimneys unloading everyday their dromedaries
>   in seraglio —
> pajamas who step in leaps and bounds
>
> These are
> more than *just*
> *moteefs* to be dealt with in the film and "integrated" into a
>   poem:
>
> *a.* children's tin band playing
> *b.* Makeba.
> *c.* wife's murder (?)
> *d.* hero's enemy
>
> ¡Xotho is the language of hell where one must always
> refill the bottles of hooch stolen from
> the closets with water
> that will not kiss you unless you give it five dollars
>
> Unless you first spit
> before you enter the door
> Zululand of my soul you come to meet your Father
> Dance playing the white goats as sousaphones

A more recent, unpublished poem, "The Price of Gold (Again) on the Market Today at $754.10," considers the relationships of value between "civilization" and the historical and economic hardship of mining in geographically remote locations. He writes:

>   it isn't Suzanne Pratt who announces it this time
>
> but Suzie Gharib (Beauty takes the acrid taste
>   from ill-gotten gain)   Ebony torsos of miners
> swathed in sweat
> somewhere in Nelson Mandela's homeland
>
> (Etruscan Minoan Assyrian Egyptian) Here I might be found
>
> strumming a mandolin or perhaps caressing a mannequin's nakedness

> "The on-line world   getting even more crowded"   "*Alors
>   avancer transporter esclaves à l'intérieure*"   On the way
> to *Malebolge*   The *Sol   escudos   corazon   jaguar   vasija*
>   — *O royaume!*   My *Hetáiras*
>   *passetemps* in the ellipse

Both poems infuse the everyday with a sense of historical continuity, cultural narratives interweaving in the play of poetic art. The "surreal" experience of the poem exists insofar as distinct cultural formations are associated in close range of the poet's sense of delight and curiosity. Torregian's artistic affinities are integrated with an understanding of the coexistence of diverse phenomena that only poetry can bring into awareness through careful (and playful) association. The powerful and unassuming voices he provides to readers are, indeed, undercut with a profound sense of the absurd. And yet, such absurdity comes not so much from the poem as from the complex weave of contemporary life and attention to it.

It is not difficult to imagine how the life of a French surrealist in North America can be hard to sustain. In efforts to support his writing over the years Torregian has worked at a number of jobs, notably contributing to the development of the aforementioned African American Studies program at Stanford in the 1960s and '70s with anthropologist St. Clair Drake. He bonded with Drake over their connection to the Négritude poets, and as a result of his studies in African cultures, Torregian was invited to present lectures on African literature and philosophy. He worked with Drake until 1975, when Drake retired and Torregian's position was eliminated during a highly sensitive political moment. He found employment in the public libraries of Menlo Park until the death of his mother triggered agoraphobia. For many years he could not leave his house, forcing him to live primarily on SSI disability.

Over the years that I have corresponded with Torregian, first in the Bay Area and now at his home in Stockton, California, I have been grateful for the view of the world he has maintained, for it is deeply humane and learned. And his humor slices through the darker realities of his life, which include poverty, racial adversity, and isolation. He has moved several times since I've known him, landing in Stockton several years ago. There he endures the Central Valley's long summers. He survives on very little, sharing an apartment with his cats. But I remember how we once met in San Francisco soon after Fred Rogers, the creator of *Mr. Rogers' Neighborhood*, had passed away. Torregian expressed sincere sadness, recalling how his children had grown up entranced by the educator's public persona. Listening to Torregian's recollections led me to reflect on my own experience of childhood, and turned my attention to Mr. Rogers with great sympathy.

In this way Torregian can spin the world without the glaze of irony. This is perhaps what is the most surreal about him: he embraces the full force of things with a curiosity and a sincere persistence that helps increase perspectives of the truly strange cultural carnivals of celebrity and loneliness, public action and private pain. While he is a man (like many) who has devoted a life to poetry for little monetary return (his few awards include the Frank O'Hara Award for Poetry in 1968), his evaluations of popular culture, contemporary politics, and social policy, along with a rich, Euro-American poetic tradition, contribute an extraordinary vision. Sotère's compulsive devotion to the art of writing proposes an intensity of purpose that evades easy categorization. He is in the world on his own terms, yet we gain as readers by his perseverance in them.

Dale Smith

Originally Published: March 17, 2010

http://www.poetryfoundation.org/article/238946

A N(otA) B(ene)

This book is hereby dedicated to the Artist/Painter Tarun Bedi and his lovely wife Paola Barbieri, my friends for many years—it has been a long time coming.

As the surrealist artist, poet, and impressario Edwards James, who was a driving force behind the International Surrealist Exhibition, London, 1936, and a patron of many surrealist artists, once said of himself, "There are surrealists who are not necessarily affiliated with the group, who do not know that they are surrealists."

Such is the case with my Friend and one whom I call "Brother", *Tarun Bedi.* — T A R U N B E D I — His ancestry emanates from the marvellous reaches of *Simla* which mirrors the Swiss Alps in the Punjab region of India; he is now an Italian citizen living with his wife, Paola Barbieri (a Doctor of Psychology) in Rome, Italy. [Of note, Tarun acted the part of a mystic-wanderer flute-player in the first segment, entitled "*Histoire d'eaux*" and directed by Bernardo Bertolucci, of the omnibus film *Ten Minutes Older: the Cello* (2002).]

Tarun's paintings and collages date from the 1960's into the 1980's. He has exhibited in London, Milan, Paris, and in the United States. At the moment Tarun is unable to paint, or make collages, but the poetic evidence of his artwork can be found at *www.tarunbedi.com,* which has been generously funded by the late Ray Burns (*trainweb.com*), who was a lover of the poetry of trains.

I stay in touch with Tarun and Paola. My communication is through the post ("real mail", that is) or the telephone.

Sotère Torregian

[To the left <top> is a painting by Tarun Bedi's father, painter and poet Ishwar Chitarkar (Ishwar Singh Bedi), depicting a scene from the Punjab epic *Ranjha and Hir*. <Bottom> Tarun Bedi as he appears as as the flute-player in Bertolucci's segment film "*Histoire d'eaux*".]

For Chitrakar, Poet & Painter of the Punjab

> *Comme l'ambre, le muse, le benjoin et l'encens*
> *Qui chantent les transports de l'esprit et des sens*
> ("Like amber, musk, benzoin and incense / Which
> chant the transports of spirit and of sense")
> – Charles Baudelaire, *Correspondances*

O Singer! the mountains valleys and streams
still receive   the call of your flute

and She whom you love   is absent   from your embrace
                              yet hears the call

magical notes of your flute in her soul

It is but this material world with its bonds
of Space and Time   that separates you
              from the lover's union

Here I receive its echoes and transmit them to the ages
                         to come

                    19. *x*. AD2010

A Woman I Met in Trafalgar Square June 25th 1936 (Five Years Before I Was Born)

YOU HAVE EXTENDED your hand to me, that of a stranger. You've seen my mustache is not green, and that I don't abide in the Himalayas. Also, that I revile weapons, their users and those fascinated by them. (One can "look at" the art of weaponry and yet one must distinguish these implements *are* meant to kill fellow human beings and/or animals as "sport"). And yet I have sat with a coterie of hunters, who constantly boast having killed this or that "game". And it was when I was a child I wished for "magical powers" to revive all those poor hunted creatures, whose lives were vicariously taken by hunters. (I wanted to effect this in the name of my dog, "Princie", whom I wanted to elect as President of The United States—or, at best, "star hitter" for the New York Yankees.) If we went right now into the midst of the Sahara, *i.e.*, South of the Sahara, we'd have a bit of a difficult time trying to explain the *Yankees* and the rules of baseball to the Blue Men Nomads living there in the desert. But I'm sure we'd be welcome, as it is the custom to show hospitality to the stranger, a tradition amongst the inhabitants, both Arab and Berber, of the Magreb and elsewhere, say, in the Middle East.

It took me nearly two hours to get out of the house this morning. I had no "idea" where French Literature was going, or, for that matter, where I was "going"... but, then, I found out. You ask if I have a "secret"? Well, yes, I do. I don't fall down the stairs each morning when I'm awake. *Et quand je suis avec les jeunes.* And when amongst the young, I am young and when amongst the old, I am then become old. When amongst Porcini mushrooms, I too am a Porcini (mushroom, that is). I hope that isn't too surprising as I confess it has been the longest time since I've had a grilled cheese sandwich. It made much for philosophy in the "old days". And yes I have travelled to the borders of madness and sipped from its stream. I return there, there being clothed naked against the ritual of my shadow, seen at the window, putting on pajamas.

3,754 people have forgotten to write me today! Of course, they did need to know me first. As the eighty-eight year old Pontiff of the Church, I haven't asked you yet what your favourite colours are. Do you like me, for instance, in this flame-coloured chasuble or in the peacock one? Now I haven't as yet seen you wear red socks which delight me on girls. Now, there's a clue of sorts. I'm happy I'm not in the "mainstream". Don't have to sit and fidget in the "war room" anymore or say the word "daunting" at every opportunity. I'm happy to quote Winnie The Pooh and say, "Ah, it's 9.15 A.M., time already for an end to chicanery." You will note, as I haven't returned from China, my name isn't Marco Polo (so-called inventor of spaghetti) although surrounded on all sides by swamps, the world reported brilliant colourations of sunrise and sunset.

Sometime *circa* AD2002, or maybe not

Amtrak Update — For Ray Burns

> *Toute ma marchandise est débarquée et j'attends le départ d' une grande caravanne pour m'y joindre.* ("All my goods are landed, and I expect the start of a great caravan for me to join.")
> — Arthur Rimbaud, *Correspondance*, Tadjoura, 28 February 1886
>
> "*It's got to be about trains* " — Ray Burns*

I'm not riding on a train tonight but I could be
                               like *Hercule*
      Poirot
         on the Orient Express   who doesn't know
he's riding with a host of murderers

in the majors this month alone

"felt like I just carried that out there"

If I lie on my left side perhaps
there will be more *ideas?*
reboots   for   far-reaching   effects   *Ach!*

The phone —*ringing at 11.00 P.M.?* It had better be
a voice belonging to a woman
no less beautiful than Helen of Troy at the other end
         But when I finally get there the phone stops ringing

La Plata, Mo.   Train-web   A long way from meeting
    myself vagabond en route on the Overland Trail Express
and the pillage of Iraq's art treasures

Ecco!   the fine line
    between madness   and genius

When my "train of thought" moves across the Abyss
all the passengers within are all the women I have ever loved

                                  24 Sept. AD2010

---

*It was during the preparation of this book that I discovered the sad news of the passing of Raymond James Burns (October 7, 1942 - July 22, 2014), a constant, generous friend, whom I will truly miss.

Laura

> *Forse anchor ti serva Amore ad un tempo*
> *migliore... Et in questa trapasso sospirando...*
> ("Perhaps Love is saving you for a better
> time... And with this sighing I continue...")
> – Petrarca, *Di pensier in pensier*

Each time I enter your domain
                            I'm lost again
as a stray dog straightening his shirt-front
a refugee from Taÿgetos
                  (you won't find it
                  on your map)

You release this child of Siné
from the manacles with which
his hands are bound

As the opus expands in directions I hadn't
anticipated
                      As you draw the curtains with their
magical design which can only be found
in the weave of carpets from *Tabriz*
that interdict the dawn

Already on your forehead
rests the diadem of the *Cinquecento*

(You wear Artemis' sandals)

Even "with results not readily available"

Having moved from here
      (as you once told me was your ultimate intent)
         "to begin a new life"

It is still my desire that lingers there
as I pass now that abode which was once yours

        As over the span
        of innumerable miles

comes the *suspiro* (sigh) of my Brother as he reads these lines

                AD2010

Passeggiata

Deh fammiti vedere in ogni loco!
("O make me see in every place!")
– Michelangelo Buonarroti,
Rime (*XVI secolo*)

My toothbrush's missing   I didn't realize

I'd already packed it
in my overnight kit bag to plan
   for my visit to my Daughters' in Morgan Hill

              As I sit here I have
"The Harmony of The Spheres" at my command

There isn't any *code*
        to "The Da Vinci Code"   All one has to do
is to disappear — into the Mona Lisa's gaze

              There one will retrace
Guru Nanak's footprints moving from past to future
"to the stars and beyond"

The *Black Diaspora* * — there's no reason to stop there

O I am still the same person
who met Paola Barbieri regal as a Persian princess
by the fountain in White Plaza (Stanford) *ancora la sua
esistenza la sua influenza nei fenomeni* **

Can you believe it? It's 8.25 A.M. And I haven't as yet
made my first phone call A leaf squats on my carpet
                                          by the door

Beauty of Woman shepherds us *à L'infini* to Infinity

---

*The Black Diaspora, term applied to the dispersion of African Peoples throughout the Mediterranean and the New World, during the classical period as well as the period of European Colonialism.

***ancora la sua esistenza la sua influenza nei fenomeni,* It., "yet his existence and influence in the phenomena"

Tableau for Tarun Bedi & for Kabir Bedi

I don't see you galloping   out of the tableau of
   Aaron Copeland's *Appalachian Spring,* but I am sure

you are there

                    The best pants
are those which are more comfortable rather
than admirable   to the camp-followers of Bollywood

We don't hear any more from the "hungry generation"
   (of Srinivas Krishna & Co.) George Montgomery once
      lauded *circa* 1963 — New York, Lower East Side)

Stopped in the middle of the poem to create yet a new one

Taking along Cinnamon Altoids rather than the usual
licorice   STOLICHNAYA
                          Auguri is only for
rare occasions, given the present state of Yours Truly's
finances *Da indi, sì come viene ad orecchia dolce armonia...**

As per the alert O steersman here we speak
Weltanschauung
                I don't have to worry
at a barbeque about what to wear Ladies I don't
eat red meat — which should be good news for

Gnus gramophones
                      In Africa men and beasts
are not merely bodies (Guru Nanak would agree)

Before emerging "out"
of doors
           apply my makeup a-la-Charlie Chaplin in *The Tramp*
  and *into* the world (I'm tempted to say the *void)*

As the first original Kabir once said:
"I'm like a fish out of water flapping in the world"

---

*Da indi, sì come viene ad orecchia dolce armonia..., It., "By then, as to the ear comes sweet harmony..." - Dante, *Paradiso*, Canto XII.

Paola Barbieri
— © Tiziana Bedi

On Paola's Birthday

for Paola Barbieri and Tarun Bedi, Rome, Italy

> *J' écris ton nom*
> ("I write your name")
> – Paul Éluard, *Liberté*

You have it still   the same joyous
expectancy, saying "Ciao, Sotère!" on the phone
You are the same Persian beauty in a sari encountered
      beside the white fountain in the Plaza years ago

              It's true
"my life" hasn't become any easier
My beard's shaved "because of the heat"

          (ah, global warming)
but mostly because there are too many bearded
"neocons" yapping away on the TV news

5 A. M. — An anonymous lover
pulls away in his car after a possible tryst with a neighbor

The poet's plaint ("They flee from me that sometimes
did me seek with naked foot, stalking in my chamber")
      is still mine —

                              —Yet   encore *Le Rive Gauche*
The Siné-Saloum delta   flows on with the Mediterranean
in my blood   with the voices of countless ancestors

As Pygmalion's art once captured
                                  G a l a t e a
her feminine grace and ageless elegance
       sculpted in mid-air

So these hands
           retrace still
                      your form

                                             9th August AD2005

L' Inconnu Arshile Gorky
(The Unknown Arshile Gorky)

> *Le sang est á la pointe de la vue comme d'une*
> *épée* ("Blood is the rapier's point of view")
> – André Breton-René Char-Paul Éluard,
> *Ralentir travaux*

They have killed the Indians and mocked the Blacks
And all that is left here
are but shiny cartoons

And all the sweet ladies and all the sweet gentlemen,
after eating art like the steak from a recipe
    bulging with fat—
they announce themselves as "serious" cooks!

This culture's a recipe culture. Nothing springs
    from within
even feeling is acquired by them
from a recorded recipe.
This is a culture without a heart.
Its god is a technique god
                        but the image
                         is dust.

A tool in itself cannot create,
it needs a hand behind it

My art is my salvation.

And so here we are on America's streets,
picking up kidney beans!

                                                    6 July AD2014

Transcription adapted from Arshile Gorky's own words in his letter to his sister Vartoosh, 1947.

(*These are as words taken out of my own mouth.* — S.T.)

For Arshile Gorky, the Lost Newark Airport Murals

> *dans les ruines indestructibles de son silence*
> ("in the indestructible ruins of his silence")
> –Aimé Césaire, *"Lynch II"*, *Soleil cou coupé*

Of those young women seated there
in the Newark Airport seating room (some idly chewing gum)
their legs crossed exposed
      through nylon stockings
          (which legs would you have chosen?)
as that little boy myself was tempted always to look
up their skirts and enfold myself
in them as in a teepee

As the cigar-smoke of Wagnerian Bureaucrat judges ruminates on
"acceptable art" filtered through terrible nightmares
            of men in white pilot caps holding me
captive in a checkered taxi cab, which speeds away
from my mother and father in a car following us in mad pursuit

The Black shoe shine boy flicks his polishing rag
           corner of Broad and Market Streets

In the movie theatres Indians in war bonnets
bite the dust on the "silver screen"
as but an ornament
                         for the whims of the White Man
whom holds the globe —O Brave New World!—
in his hands   As each day I take refuge
    in my grandmother's apartment   and seat myself there
on the Oriental carpet from Baghdad
                             waiting for it to take flight

                                                 1978

Arshile Gorky—"Study for *Agony*"

> *Glace de ténèbres...*
> ("Ice of darkness...")
> – André Breton,
> *Clair de terre*

Worth the long lingering trajectory
of a young woman's sweetest caresses

Secrets of Cuzco's gold   in your eyes
you knew the time of the unveiling
the rending of the temple's view felt in your veins
as it traveled almost without stop
                      to the place

        where you now found yourself
Antics of circus clowns not any more miserable than the rest of us
thus for me everything comes clearly into view

O Qasidas and jarchas!   O of Mozárabic Al-Ándalus!
You are made whole and new   quickened
      to enter the current

of this light   domestic animals and their pasturage
inventions of gunpowder the compass of paper and printing

the discovery that the centre of the Universe revolves
about the sun

It will never be finished this our need ever to be considered

        your fervent gaze that continues to radiate upon
                              all things

        June, 1978
        Menlo Park, California

The Young Arshile Gorky Astride his White Stallion Overlooking the Ancient Site of *Sourp Khatcha*

> *Alors la devise charmante de l'éclair*
> *Descend sur la bannière des ruines*
> ("Then the charming motto of lightning bolt
> Descends upon the banner of ruins")
> –André Breton, *Clair de terre*

The Empress of Silence
dons her cloak of invisibility as she defers
      her great cloak to you

O Friend!
As you gallop forth on the plain this morning
you bring your mount to a sudden halt
above the heights overlooking the ancient church
of SOURP KHATCHA!
            It is the morning of the world
which opens for you

First or last
A gasp of ten thousand
            in one
bated breath

      You prayed, "O never leave me, my ancestral
SOURP KHATCHA" which you took within your embrace
the moment

before Marconi's radio was invented   its waves moving steadily
                                in the ether

            (though no one as yet had discovered its sound)

Within you conversations
of the past present and future overlapped in your mind
Dowagers over tea considering the inevitable lack of "initiative"
        amongst today's artists "on the dole"
in whose minions I find myself

        Your darksome shadow hums to yourself

Percy Grainger's "(English) Country Gardens" only in America

Long incomprehensible idlenesses welding each painting
to your need in Exile
        The garage your workshop in Connecticut
                        —   great gateway to
"the analogical world"

                                        1978

"Child of an Idumean Night" by Arshile Gorky

Je t'apporte l'enfant d'une nuit d'Idumée!
("I bring you the child of an Idumean night!")
– Stéphane Mallarmé, *Don du poeme*

Of the sacred and the profane
our respective likenesses greet each other to exchange
                                      ardour

    — A common obsession / Armenia's disappearance —

into gamelan flourescence   of cocktail waitresses
    asking questions as to our preferences

Even you, my Arshile, would have said as I do
Pamela Sue Martin ("Fallon" of *Dynasty*) I steal into Babylon for you
For just one moment   To see you also
as "Nancy Drew" undraped in the nude
You made the most of ostracism O my Mentor

Today's bread
without body testifies
As a witness in the wilderness

O speak you damnable hunters long vanished
into the trees' nightmare tapestries!
—*Speak* you incarnadine steering wheel of the 1948 Ford auto!
Numinous *faits accomplis*

    Arshile! You never quite "mastered" French be that as it may
But one nuance of the language of the Haïs* is worth 30 Gallic utterances
worth all the delights laden
in Omar Khayyám's mobile garden in Isphahan

1978

---

*Language of the Haïs, the Armenian language. Armenians call themselves Haïs and their land Hayástan. What is now Anatolian Turkey was once in the realm of the ancient Armenian kingdom.

The View From Occupied Alcatraz
for John "Tito" Gerassi

Would this wall   have crossed the meridian
                                       as Dido's woe
upon the departure of Aeneas
                             As the last gasp
of those buried
in subterranean   vaults of sand
     Before the sunlight was shut out
forever from their eyes   *O Floating-Island Eyesore!*

Your spectre on the shores   so men and women tattoo themselves
now "Dean" on his arm & "Marie" on hers (rather, the woman's leg)

But the unseen tattoo that I wear is A L C A T R A Z
                              On days when I see it and
on days when I don't
                       One with the mechanical *Zora*
     in a boardwalk booth handing out her fortune cards
Another in the Wax Museum
     displaying the Execution of *Atahualpa*
with Pizarro in attendance as victor
                                    Among its most recent visitors
Clint "Dirty Harry" Eastwood & Rosemary "Queen of Romance" Rodgers
attending a guided tour of *Dante's Inferno*
whose hooded processioners superimposed by the KKK in the movie
                                         "The Spanish Earth"

continues to roll until the reel spins off the projector's arm
falling down endlessly down the numberless steps pummeling
within the empty echoes of a hollow skull

                    The skull of an Indian child that comes to rest
at the bottom of the main cellblock's cellar

                        I continue to hear the repeat of its descent
in my sleep and in my waking

          I see it in the teepee that my young daughter has drawn

          I see Alcatraz
and *I hear Alcatraz* skip a beat in my heart as the woman doctor
applies the stethoscope (it's cold)

   I see Alcatraz reflected in the store windows that I pass
In the silver dollars geysering from one arm bandits in Vegas

Its sound is contained in an ancient volcano erupting
In the syllables uttered in Hello

                        The tour boat approaches
Its passengers strain their necks to "see"
the tiny Alcatraz bracelet charms in the gumball machines

The Lady of the Lake   from out of the sea's darkness
     holds aloft her torch
But no light enters

                      Not so far
flutter pages of TV comedic scripts with jokes about Alcatraz
in the wind above the clouds

All I did not know   in the continuity of my day
Activities that filled my life with lists of "Things to do"
     Even as there was no necessity for your knowing
Revealed now   with disbelief   you enter   Now

the chambers of my wound
               Alcatraz Island
                         viewed from afar

San Francisco, 1971

ENTRECHAT
Homage to TEHLIRIAN!

Here   the birds sing   There inside you the River Araxes

flows on inside you   all that has ever escaped
       my pen   *The Internationale*   plays on   its *Appel*
to the oppressed of the world   AS YOU STEP FORWARD
              ONTO THE WORLD STAGE   avenging angel
In your wake   lost   sketches
           of Arshile Gorky's "Charred Beloved"
The sword of Vartan companions the Rose of Yerevan
in a *threnos*   Abducted Africans on the Atlantic Passage   the
      clanging of their chains   drops of sweat glisten
mixed with blood from the Agony in the Garden of Gethsemane

O sable hair of Armenian maidens severed from my kisses

AS THERE ON A SIDE STREET IN BERLIN my doppelgänger's
in your shadow   still with a tap on the shoulder
        of the unsuspecting sauntering "Turkish Gentleman"
Aficionado of slaughter

                A single shot fired point blank not by one
          but by a million or more spectral dead
Mothers Daughters Sons Fathers Brothers Sisters
                                      Innocents of Van
There in unison   stand as well
My French Surrealist *compères* who squeeze the trigger of your pistol
alongside you   at that moment   *My Soghomon Tehlirian!*

At that moment as the obese, slaughterous Turk
Talaat Pasha falls headfirst in front of you
before he can even think
when or where to go to take his next fart

                                               AD2006

*   *   *

(In Remembrance of those slaughtered Armenians who constitute one quarter of my ancestral blood.)

*   *   *

Entrechat: Fr., Ballet term: a leap in which the dancer repeatedly crosses his legs and sometimes beats them together.

*   *   *

So I envisioned the avenging angel, Soghomon Tehlirian (1896-1960) as he appeared before the mass murderer Talaat Pasha, who gave the order for the expulsion and eventual execution on the Long March of Van 1915 of a million or more Armenian citizens of Turkey. Soghomon would have been a youth of 19 or so at the time, witness to the murder of his parents and other members of his family and friends of the Armenian Community along the path of the Van Death March, which is commemorated worldwide every April.

Tehlirian, disguised as an upstanding businessmen, caught up with the mass murderer Talaat Pasha, in Berlin, 1921, and there shot him, avenging the deaths of over one million innocent Armenians. He is enlisted here as one of the perpetual heroes of the poet and posthumously nominated as amongst the surrealist ranks for his actions.

Soghomon Tehlirian passed away in the Bay Area of California in 1960.

S.T.

For the French National Assembly and Its Resolution Inditing the Turkish Nation for Its Massacre of the Armenians in 1915

for M. Jean-Louis Armand

Stretched out   the measuring line
Tetendit funiculum   *Travois*
   Of The Nameless   continues on:
Van / Guernica   *Beirut / Beslan*
October (29th) and a reminder it will be Daylight Savings
                             Time in America

D'Anthès' bullet*   *The Wall of Respect* in Chicago
still endures though eroded by vandals

         The "emptiness" is now filled

That annihilates the distance
and separated the phenomenon
                      Sayat Nova ("trouvère
                              arménien"
   The Frenchman on the bus seated next to me recognizes
   the name as I hold the book in my hand)

who sang Ashough's descant of his beloved's sable hair

Unmarked graves   of the *Communards* lie annealed
in the heart of Paris
                (where the monument to the Emperor
Napoleon was pulled down)

ô histoire   (beautè d')   Immaculée   Ilibagiza

A.   Of the lineage of *Amirian*   Patricia
      Named her firstborn girl child *ANAHID* (Armenian
              counterpart to the goddess Aphrodité)

B.   Where in my veins   their blood of *Erzérum*
        meets with that of the *Siné-Saloum*

      How many times
(in a lifetime)   must I   rise
out of bed   and return to it again

And *Avedis* means Hope (*l'éspoire en arménien*)

Petrarca at *Vaucluse* :   *ed io dico forse ancor*
ti serva Amore   ad un tempo migliore
                        That is,
When you return *My Muse*
with the splendour of the *Château de Vareilles*
             still shining in your eyes

And here as a discarded newspaper lying in the street
are illustrations on an upturned page   *of keys*

Keys to open what doors?

O locks to doors which no longer exist!   for ghastly hands

Ah, Montesquieu!... a time of ignorance
        "committed
even the greatest evils   without
            the least scruple"

Is this not true? "Pedro" (AKA K ____ ğlu)
rode the Zephyr   on AMTRAK in 1976 in disguise en route
      fearing the Armenian Red Army
  a Turkish dignitary
as a "Mexican Rancher" tourist to New York
      and to whom I asked if he had a lovely daughter
I might marry...

Stretched out   the measuring line

Ennui de la ténèbre   the tree the air the light & co.

For those who would ask   A love song
as much as   any other / *1739 The Declaration*
of the Rights of Man / Woman / And Citizen

It is true *France*   that voices   Ransom
Now   extends
                enlivens
                        embraces

That Right
cette raison   as yet

To
All the world

                        12—14 October, AD2006

Notes :

*D'Anthès' bullet... Baron d'Anthès slew the Russian poet Puskin, his wife's brother-in-law, during a pistol duel in 1837.

Sayat Nova, Armenian Ashough, Troubadour poet, 1712-1795. His tomb located in Tbilisi (Tiflis), Georgia; works translated into Persian, Georgian, Azerbaijani, and, in 2006, French. Sergei Parajanov's *Sayat Nova* (1968), an ethnic-Armenian film, when released in the U. S. was retitled *The Color of Pomegranates.*

Unmarked graves of the Communards: Revolutionaries in the Paris uprising and Paris Commune of 1871, after the Franco-Prussian War, who were slaughtered by the French military.

Immaculée Ilibagiza: Female survivor of the 1994 *Rwanda Genocide.* Author of *Left to Tell, Discovering God Amidst The Rwanda Holocaust*, a memoir, translated from the French, AD2006.

As I Set My Pen To Paper Today (Our Dialogue Continues)
for Mlle. Louise Burchill

> *... d'avoir en mon coeur*
> *le sang d' un autre coeur*
> ("... to have in my heart
> the blood of another heart")
> —Paul Éluard, "*Vivre*"

"Ultimately the beauty of life is to transcend"
My words   come to you becoming
something
       "Other"
            (l'Autre)
                    Are you
my pearl   Or am I your oyster?
Can we both
       be awake and at the same time
dawn in Texas?

The web of gossamer you give I turn into a ladder

We   the inheritors of cuneiform

If you hold one of the clay tablets
   in your hand
it becomes a dancing girl
         that swirls into Arabic writing

الفنجان

                a fish in your desert waiting
to become a seahorse

      I pass
on this Flame

              of *L'Hôtel des Invalides*   Paris
from my palm   to yours

Your dress of diamond-shimmers *sagesse* ("wisdom")
      just crossed   your threshold

And except for the sunflower
                (*Le Tournesol*)

                    all countries then
                          become obsolete

I still speak your name as I did

From the very first   so many times now
in my thoughts
              that you hear me each time

As it occurs even as far away as you are

                                    –Sotère
                                    December, 1996

Note: الفنجان *Ar., Feejan,* or *finjan,* a small, round, handle-less cup

For Antoinette In Autun, France

O my muse
I have no country
I take for my standard for battle
that same ensign Emiliano Zapata bore.

That of Nuestra Señora   Our Lady Of Guadalupe
The soil of Tepayac   my sacred ground
and that of all humanity.

I sometimes have difficulty putting all the "pieces
of the puzzle" together, for that matter
But eventually   all lead to Castalia.

Some 15 or so odd books testify I walked this Earth.
          Names of innumerable kinsmen and kinswomen
are inscribed
              in Slave Auction logs of America's History.

My Lady   to whose hand I make my pilgrimage *

Make of it what you will
On the nation's "Memorial Day"   my salute
goes forth —To Garfield, whose sole allegiance is to the refrigerator.

                              31ˢᵗ May, AD2005

Note:

Pilgrimage: Pelegrinus, voyageur, en un lieu sainte: le main de ma femme qu' est la route de l'amour fou , Fr.

("Pelegrinus, voyager, in a holy place: the woman's hand which is the road to mad love")

*   *   *

(Gloss For Antoinette In Autun, France)

A French poet once said that for him The Poem was the only homeland he acknowledged.

But it is I that acknowledge the same. I no longer have a homeland. The homeland remains The Poem. Yet the poem itself remains also as *Terra Incognita.* I travel there, expecting to settle, but find I am still wandering in unknown territory. Once "at home" in the poem I find myself lost in unknown terrain, traveling still ("South" — — "North" — — ? —)

The things of this world no longer satisfy.

I drink water or wine and am thirsty again. I satisfy my hunger only momentarily; in the evening I search for more food.

Ainsi, La Femme. Woman is the source of all stable culture (she is there in unstable culture as well, roaming with nomads in the Harmattan,* braving the Sahara or the Sahel of Africa). The men are too busy killing each other or engaged in the hunt for survival. There are some exceptions (men not engaged in savageries), of course, such a man as Plato — we will never know if he intentionally or inadvertently killed a man; there is the testimony of Van Gogh left in marvellous paintings, or in his letters to his brother Theo; the supreme poet and mystic Ibn Al Arabi; the Englishman John Keats (whose grave resides in the Protestant Cemetery in Rome, "Here Lies One Whose Name Was Writ in Water"); the beatific Mozart; Beethoven, whose true home was not Germania but — along with Hölderlin — Olympus. Yet the *matrix* remains, I repeat, for all established culture, *Woman:* She *(Elle)* who inspires; she who befriends; she who cultivates the arts.

The historical symbol of France (*La France*) has always been the Goddess Ceres,** who seeds and nourishes the Earth.

Notes to Gloss:

Poet André Frénaud (1907-1993): the *Poème* as homeland, "Où est mon pays? C'est dans le Poème." His first collection of poetry *Les rois mages* ("*The three wisemen*," 1943) was praised by Paul Éluard, Louis Aragon and René Char.

**Harmattan:* Storm of wind and sand that occurs on the coast of former French West Africa. This northeasterly wind blows from the Sahara Desert into the Gulf of Guinea between the end of November and the middle of March (winter).

***Ceres:* Goddess of agriculture, grain crops, fertility and motherly relationships; Roman version of the Greek goddess Demeter.

In the Silence (After Your Voice)
for Antoinette

(Then) the silence comes after your voice *My Muse*
speaking with me on the phone filling itself
with bird calls meadows Spring flowers and castles
   in the clouds   *Voila!*

The bystander viewing this all from above   is myself
three minutes after our conversation's over
The pot of macaroni   *rears*   like an untamed horse
Hey! WHOA!   then begins to croon

                                          I finally discover
in that space what was really inside Napoleon's coat (David's
portrait of him "hand-held-in-waistcoat"   the enigma of
which has been debated for years amongst the cognoscenti)
actually it's a little man 1 ¼ inches tall hidden inside
   there, sitting beside a campfire   cooking soup

   As the smoke was never detected *no one ever guessed
what was really going on inside*   *the Emperor's waistcoat*

Our words this time over the phone had sparred
but quite amicably   over "social issues"

                In the interim a spider's building its web
a single gossamer thread that can go on potentially forever

                                          AD2005

The Poet Speaks Through the Painter's *Voice of Fire*
for Rosanna Mombelli

Et dans mon coeur veillait comme une lampe votre sourire
("And in my heart ensured as a lamp your smile")
– Léopold Sédar Senghor, *Éthiopiques*

As my love reaches and crosses continents   To venture
with its seven-league boots
of Mayakovsky
With its stride   of the giant Paul Bunyan
but in defiance of "loggers"   their *hubris* in felling trees
and past the stink that emits from
jubilant cigars after their wretched deeds

But also with new brides' feet of doves
to witness

Amongst children of Armenia   orphaned by the great earthquake
in their country   given refuge in the heart of
    Fidel's Cuba

then moving across   arroyos and canyons

with a bit of that Red Sea parted by Moses
used for a fan to ease my body heat
stopping for a moment to pause
        at the site where Emiliano Zapata
was gunned down in ambush by Federales in a hail of bullets
at the Hacienda de San Juan in Chinameca

Yet making myself small enough to fit into
the envelope you open with anticipation

              As you dress yourself in your boudoir
ô bien-amié! readying yourself for work   Is it Monday
or Tuesday in Brazil
As this morning you fit on your black bra and black
     lace panties   garter belt   and black stockings
slipping on your high-heels (not "stilleto" but moderate ones
     more or less)   a dash of *L'Air du Temps*
with you throughout your day

Traversing the Transatlantic cable connecting
inchoate voices of men and women in a babel of languages
that invoke   judgements and preconceptions
that imprison the speakers... *"But you! — you! —
never do"* ...(this or that)... *"It's the same." "No, it's not
the same" etc.*   The cacophany   rises and subsides

          As in the silence as *voyeur* I find myself
viewing the shoe dangle from the lovely young
woman's foot as she sits intent at her work
     behind her desk   at Lloyd's Bank (its white stallion
rears) in São Caetano do Sul

As I adjust my Jean Valjean feather-warrior pants
again and let
the primal wound   of desire
       take me   where it will

                                  21 April AD1990

Note to "The Poet Speaks Through the Painter's' Voice of Fire'": As to the painting, "Voice of Fire" by Barnett Newman, an old friend from my New York days, it apparently caused a raucous when it was displayed in Canada in 1989. The painting on exhibit was appraised for around one million dollars to the objection of some Canadian critics who did not even grant the painting as being worthy as art.

      *   *   *

This poem is dedicated to the then Ms. Rosanna Mombelli, a young Brazilian woman, whom I met by chance during her visit to the United States in 1988. She reconfirmed for me *le coup de foudres* ("the bolt of lightning") which I thought had been absent from my sensibilities for some time, and the impact of her luminous presence has remained with me to this day.

                       S.T.

Rue de l'Abbè-de-l'Épèe
(For One Who Resides There)

for Michel Deguy and for Wilson Baldrige

— — *Finalement!* — Finally, it came to me this morning, while all naked in the bath like Archimedes

    All *hommage* to you who reside at the *rue de l'Abbé-de-l'Épée!*
        I can say
   with all distinction (though the world covers it with scorn rather than with honour) I am interrupted in all my plans, wherever and whenever I have to go, by Poetry

    I go to find that Fifth Musketeer (male or female?) of Summer leaving a pavonian cloak over the horizon

    And, yes, Walt is again walking with me albeit invisibly on this unpaved road

        "where the grove of Artemis and reliquary of
      the goddess the winding stream amidst glowing fields of
      the Rhine itself   or the rainbow is being described"

   I have here but the dust of the Valley Of The San Joaquin (Even as I think upon Monet's locomotive smoke at
              the Gare Saint-Lazare and the
      women who waited there who are no more)

   The Milesian wine is blessed

I still hold that it is the steps which led Alexander to the altar
of the Oracle at Thebes rather than the oracle received there
(*Process* — *process*, — rather than the end-product)...
In the fall, she said, "We will meet again and exchange photos of
our (respective) families", but she doesn't know of the long desire
I have pent up inside for her (even as she has had thus far four
surgeries on her injured shoulder which has left her writing-hand
impaired

yet she has journeyed to Oxford in the process to present
a paper on the modern temper)

—— *The Self* —— can no longer be "lost" than the wave
lose its ocean   But, yes, there can be terrible storms at sea where
the Self can be obscured   in the darkness. (It fell on my tenth birthday
in June of 1951 when, accompanied by my parents, I entered
a young pharaoh's tomb with its burial chamber – I had more interest
at the time in the display of ornate Ottoman firearms, Moorish swords
and flintlock pistols encrusted with rare gems at *The Metropolitan*.

Later on that evening

when we had returned
home a violent summer storm erupted which terrified me. I thought
it was some kind of omen. *Of what?)*

Buscando. The self lies not in the mirror but in the alcove of old
books (some of which may indeed be thought as useless now) waiting
for the one who will declare its *Open Sesame!*

Ambuscando. With its delightful Shakespearean overtones, the
writer's imaginings continuously outdone by the actualities of the media
(television, newspapers, ad agencies, etc.)...

...Yet, and yet... In the solitude of my murky room when I should
be sleeping Poetry overtakes me and announces itself
     in the Qilin* which once again comes prancing   albeit
soundlessly
         overcoming my sudden craving   for a lettuce sandwich

for the evocation of the slender arm of a young blonde woman
(Reminiscent of that magical female arm remonstrating
the Sword of Excalibur)
         who could be opening a letter

   or taking up a tea cup, for that matter
at some time in late morning

   The name Sherbrooke (Quebec) and *she who
dwells there*   (That alone could be   sufficient
     for poetry)

Epilogos

   My umbrella placed in its niche. I haven't
spoken to a soul this day   (*If,* that is,
         there *was* conversation
   with the soul — *l'âme* — then it transpired in
solitude) my walk through the mall (de-populated)

ο δεύτερος δράστης

                    Martine,
                              you perhaps have that visage
          of Diotima   whom neither of us have ever seen
— — you provide   mainstay** for your poet
allow him thus to take wing with Aeolus
    Martine   so long have I traced
the song that would assume your name!
             And it is here   sung by the Angel in Rockefeller
Center who is really Prometheus   (as a child I conceived
of him as an Angel   I, too, am a wanton
who can equally look with longing and bliss)
(*Martine*)   let your name go forth   with that of
Francesca and Artemisia   (*feed the hungry   shelter the homeless*)
                       O la *beltà*
   è ben da quel la***   "that beauty which   emanates from her"

                                            July—November, AD2007

Notes:

Walt, the allusion is to Walt Whitman (1819-1892), American poet whom the author considers a mentor.

*Qilin : Chimerical "Chinese unicorn" which when appearing portends good fortune. Said to have become visible at Confucius' birth.

ο δεύτερος δράστης, *Gr.*, "the second actor" (Ref. to Martine, a companion of the poet, who takes her place alongside the significant inspiratrices of art and poetry.)

***mainstay: Sin arrimo y can arrimo, Sp.,* ("Without and with a mainstay"), San Juan de la Cruz.

****beltà è ben da quel la, It.,* Michelangelo Buonarroti (1475-1564)

For Queen Noor of Jordan

I hear the echo   of your voice   as it searches
the ruins of Petra   Where you stand sheltered
in the portico   Your dress fluttering in the
same breeze   that heralded
the standards of Zenobia of Palmyra   O My Queen   and played

As fawns   in her bosom's bower

I hail you thus   Protectoress   Of monuments of past glories
    remaining
        in the desert!

And, yes, I know, the Siege of Chicago rages on in you

And, yes, your arms uphold and your hands touch
those made homeless by floods   in North Carolina
        and Georgia

    And along the Nile in *Nubia*   (where towering
statuaries of the Nubian pharaoh   and his consort queen
come into view at   ABU SIMBEL)
Now the Symphony rises
Now the Poem   comes into *being*   *It is now*

L'Homme – Man's eye peers through to the Infinite

The lens of the great   telescope at Mt. Palomar

    Gazelles leap on the Plain of the Serengeti   Africa

        L'Afrique encore   Offers you her dawn   mingling with

The first light   over Capernaum

In the wake of your footsteps is the footfall

        Of Balqis *(Sheba)* as she entered the Sea of Mirrors
in the Court of Solomon

Spin City "Puff Daddy" sings his rap but his isn't the enchant-
   ment of the whippoorwill or the
          meadowlark in the Spring night
—The Spring! Where once again I am Tammuz
   and she whom I love comes
      as Ishtar
to rescue me from the Abyss

And, yes, it is you who hold us in your hand mirror
as Boucher's Venus   viewing herself

And you are alone now.   As Josephine was alone in
her bed of *Tapisseries* at Malmaison

Yet peopled by a nation

   And   لعربي   (—Al Arabi,   "(I) distraught

    (again)   between"

O knowledge that has become a petting zoo!

Questquestquestquestquestquest   questquestQuest

                For Mr. Yoshiro the birds are singing
"smarter, more informed" lysts and lings could be in for heart-
stopping declines suggested Two acquaintances "more in control"
Whether you opt for   "Yclyketed" or not   Camilla
Paglia   Quentin Taratino (minus Mira Sorvino) Lou Reed or 2 Live
Crew as headlamp washers

..."Come from El-do-ra-do" (voice singing) "to fa-a-de on a
m-o-o-n lit tr-a-a-i-l..."

After 43 years   – – I give yet my
                            Red salute to space dog Laika
its satellite-urn still orbiting *our planet Earth*

Majesty   To all *voyageurs*, then!

          Now arriving   as guests given

Refuge in the oasis that   flourishes as you gaze

   "That which the
breeze
       fitfully blows
(then)   half conceals   half discloses"

     Segui il tuo corso   *e lascia*
dir le genti   ("So follow your own
road, and let others say what they will")
         — — "Now as aforetime the
maxim of the great Florentine (Dante) is mine."
               – *Karl Marx*

The masses must be drugged to perform
their hapless tasks ("jobs", "work") that are not
of their own choosing.   As the sop soaked in drugged wine
was offered to the crucified.

    All the "pop" songs we gaily sing and syncopate to
"*Goin' to Kansas City, Kansas City here I come...*" are of
       ghosts   Only a *ghost* of a remembrance therein

And, therefore, nothing really *there* to meet us
where we head...

Thus   To *begin with*   Individuation (*L., individus,* indivisible)
Rather than the paper dolls cutout of newsprint
from the Classifieds...   "In Step"

                  I have thought and
thought of those mailbags of letters
received on the *Perry Como Show* on TV way back in
the '50s   requests   for this or that song

  ..."Letters We get letters We get stacks
and stacks of letters   De-a-r-r Per-r-y
Would you be so kind   to fill a
Request and sing the songs we like best?"

"Carolina Moon (Keep Shining)"   Etc.
"Hot Diggity (Dog Diggity Boom)"!

Only shadows: *"Knoxville: Summer of 1915" "I Remember*
Paris" "Vienna, City of My Dreams" "San Antonio Rose" (Deep
within my heart lies a mel-o-dy / A song of old San
    Antone)   Ithaca and Penelope happened only once

And the *Nostoi* (the "returned ones")
show forth only tragedy   once having arrived after so
many years at sea, to their long anticipated destinations

    "8 hrs. a day?
    137,499 more to go."
    —— buildingyourfuture.com
    "Need *any* HOT ANSWERS?"
    —— hotanswers.com

    Name this *Sesame Street* character   and *get*
4 free gifts for your child.

The indigent who saw me pick up the stupid ad (for "literacy")
    would have thought I was picking up
a dollar bill from the ground
    "LEARN TO READ"
        The only *raison*
(I can see) is to acknowledge that
"sound of a different drummer" (of Thoreau)

Who
    would believe for a moment
        the craving
      to "fill the belly" could

Take precedence *over*   even desire for one's Beloved? *(Bien-amié)*

"Tell Mother I'll go to have lunch at
the Century Club"
        (*Transmission*, one of the first experimental television
          broadcasts, New York, *circa* 1930's)

Dawn On The River Moscow — Prelude *Khovanshchina* — Mussorgsky
— — shimmer of balalaikas

So verged
     the gasoline engine   To the sublime of
the *Vita Nuova*   of *il miglior fabbro* to the ritual
cutting out of the heart of an Aztec youth   the still living
victim's body thrown down the endless defile

Of steps leading to the altar of the Sun God Huitzilopochtli

And I wonder what the Greek "heroes" were "thinking" before emerg-
    ing from the bowels of the Trojan Horse inside the city gates

    It's Monday and unbelievably no one's home
Kevin's just valorized *Skye* on TV's "One Life To Live"
La votre   What does it *mean*   When
Someone says they "belong" to an other *(l'Autre)*?

Mechanicsburg (PA)   Burrough   Livestock grain soy apples
dairy   Manufacturing printing publishing machine parts   plastic
microwave fabricated steel food products Williams Grove Amuse-
ment to South Camp Hill State Correctional to East Appalachian
Trail passes to West
               As at   *Meribah*
as in the day of Massah in the desert

    ....
   The inner sanctuary   Pilgrims circumambulate
     (the) Ka'aba   seven times
              Within is Abraham's Black Stone

And Quantum   developed for   statistical study of
motion involving nuclear particles   —   Disembarkment of
the yacht "Granma" — the revolutionary struggle in Cuba... viewed as
"chimera of idealists and deluded beings"

                                        Nella prima dico siccome questa
          donna riduce in atto questa potenza (*Vit. Nu.* XXI:23)
        ("I say this because the first woman in action reduces power" - Dante*)*

    Into
the insidious sign above the gate of Auschwitz
                              "No one leaves..."
        "No one leaves..."

In the blue of the eyes of the Senior
       Citizen who finds himself
    ensconced
Opposite me   coldly staring ahead beyond
                         my Semito-Hamite guise

        This   is the enterprise
Presented before you   O Suzeraine!

That can only be transcended in a myrtle
    or laurel leaf

Equiano* has ceased his travels across the Seven Seas

    There are no more courts or
horizons for him to report to

"Wired"
(Magazine)

Now flaps   its bat-wings perched

On the porch of desire   where
shreds of lace dangle from a fugitive mistress'
                                        lingerie

Benin Guinea Virginia Montserrat Charleston
Savannah Philadelphia London   *Cogito*
                                      Ergo
              Et le grand nom de l'Afrique   Magnifies (himself)

As (he) said (he) "listened to the speech of the (White Man's) books" and
when they did not speak back to him he
learned their language (So that the books could speak *with him*)

Now arrived
(We're)   At Rengstorff House   after the "Mummy's Tomb"
has opened in the mouth of the neighbor –
        passenger on the "morning commute"
The stain on my white shirt-front
grows larger
                      Consider: on the Planet

Multimillions of interfacing voice boxes of the *vox populi*

                            Whitman never travelled with "iPod"
Earphones fastened onto his head   Instead *he journeyed*

With the recollection of Memory

The music might have been Brahms' *Variations
On A Theme By Haydn* playing on and on as he moved as a solitary in

        The Concert Hall
                inside himself

No word   comes forth   *But*
   sent-forth my word   as gonfalonier
To the morning air   Somewhere
                           You may be pensive-
ly writing a letter   or pressing a *bulla* onto
a State paper, seated at your desk

Or perhaps looking out as did once that princess of Tyre

Jaufré Rudel   voyaged after

   — — And *who knows* how long   the book
itself will endure?   Indeed, all printed pages
may vanish tomorrow in a "screen-saver" haze
upon a computer monitor
But the jewels you wear continue to augur
from your long stately gown   "An house built on rock
    or sand" an eloquence de Saussure never *poursuivre*'d

Without your spouse
                The lone cypress
       Overlooking the Pacific
windblown at Carmel-By-The-Sea   *(Dal
Libano trema e rosseggia)*

Yet peopled by a nation.

                                        April 18, 2000

Notes:

**Equiano:* (I say) in the lineage of the Carthagainian Hanno the Navigator. Within the sumptuousness of the *Salambo* of Flaubert. *The Periplus of the Erythracean Sea.* As mimetic as that original fence in Hannibal, MO. which Tom Sawyer "talked his friends into whitewashing for him." Within the fandango gaze of Lady Emma Hamilton "as nature." When we say, "We'll *liaise* (at)" *Chiffre* (Melaméd). Olaudah Equiano (Or Gustavus Vassa The African) (1745-1797) had never seen the Ocean.

"de Saussure never *poursuivre*'d" - *N.B.* Mallarmé has, in his *l'Écclestiastique*, "j'en retiens,quant à moi, un état équivoque tant que ne s'y substitue pas un naturalisme absolu ou naïf, *capable de poursuivre.*" — — *Poèmes en prose*, Stéphane Mallarmé ("I retain, as for me, an ambiguous state as long as an absolute or naïve naturalism does not take the place of its capability of continuing.")

Dal Libano trema e rosseggia ("From Lebanon trembles and is red")

*   *   *

This text was posted to Queen Noor of Jordan (the former Ms. Elizabeth "Lisa" Halaby) by way of her parent's address in New Jersey, on April 18th, AD 2000. No response was ever received by the poet, however, the poet remains an admirer of her and her life story. Her husband, King Hussein of Jordan, died in 1999. They had wed in 1978. She then had become known as *Noor Al-Hussein* ("Light of Hussein"). Today Queen Noor is the queen dowager of Jordan; she is the stepmother to King Abullah II, Hussein's first son. Noor's firstborn son had been the Crown Prince but he was stripped of his status as heir presumptive in 2004. Queen Noor has authored several books. The first was about her husband and the second, about her life, *Leap of Faith: Memoirs of an Unexpected Life* (2003), is still in print.

S.T.

For Marissa Mayer at Google

It's been ages since I uttered the name
of Eugenio Montale   Where it indicates

"Fast" on my calendar   I pencil in "Feast" instead

      I've never
          entered into a jousting session
with myself   I've just felt my head

I believe my temperature's returned to "normal"
It rises proportionately when I see a beautiful woman

With two or more together it's
a significant rise in blood pressure
    sicut compare notes with Guido Cavalcanti

This is how poems are made   We begin with Nothing
that most essential element as I began
yesterday when I had never heard your name
    spoken   And then it happened   I heard

Borodin's *String Quartet* play again (*i.e.,* in the 4th movement)

And the African Prince appeared once more
to throw his cloak over my shoulders   and disappeared
as quickly   leaving only your smile and nervous laughter

                                6 March AD2009

Temptation of the October Twilight

scrisse
("wrote")
–Giuseppi Ungaretti

Sensed   its *presence* just

          Over my shoulder between that enjambment of silhouetted
tree-boughs   The lingering look of "Beatrice Cenci" by *Guido Reni*

   I try not to notice   Go about my daily affairs   The impertinence
of its coral still there... the feel on a pendulum or hung by a hair
...Seems to *fillet* body and soul   Perhaps transmutes into *cyclops*
holding these many houses in its spell... Or an angel to give a needed
message?   I don't know which of these *it* is
   But soon the sky infused with *malana* ("octopus-ink") before I've
had time to further inquire
   That last skirmish of pink still evident   like the bared shoulder
of a woman   in a black evening gown one only sees   for a brief
instant   before she   vanishes into the crowd in the bustle in a vestibule
Then, appropriately, too, the vestibule collapses like the tallow of a
candle consumed in oblivion

   Why this evening?   Why my chevalier's gaze singled out for
dénouement?

   Am I asked again to be *Dragoman?* Could this be *so,* as there are
no more *routes,* no more caravans no more destinations   *If* I am *asked,*
then, *What* am I *asked? Ecce tetigit hoc labia tua**   And this twilight
the ember lifted by tongs to my lips?

84

......   Those passengers *à bord* a jet plane travelling into a sunset emerging as *Other (l'Autre)*   As I   move through the rooms of the house, am I any different?

A voice on the radio announces from Rwanda but the misery there only seems to coagulate the more... *Incarnadine cloak of this twilight engulfs them also*   The Dow's up 6100   Totemic thought   the welfare of the tribe antecedes   So one only receives "Thanks" for when one returns from a successful deal   But to dare venture now on the path would be as a muezzin devoid of all but a robe   As this twilight calls out like the law of talion for redress   I, its enactor, in the effort   thwarted each time   Yet still

Have tried so many times to close my door to it with indifference but to no avail

Ecce tetigit hoc labia tua , L., "See, this has touched your lips."—Isaias 6: 3-8 - Angelic thrust of live coal to the lips of the prophet, *c.f.*

"Market Correction"
for John Ashbery

> *enlaçant*
> ("embracing")
> –André Breton

That I imagine this event
gives me no reason to believe it "unreal"
The hammer dulcimer (in the form of the *santur*
        of Iran) has persisted for these
twenty centuries

Although no one can know everything for certain
in order to explain the feats of these "heroes"
a knowledge of their minds is necessary
for instance the "language" of the ant
        with that of the poet

And here the grocery list only partially complete
appears before me
    "Volatility"   characterized this day

And was it at that moment you were lifting
your *haute couture* shoes from your feet
then removed your stockings as you came in the door?

A moment perhaps Stendhal and Tolstoy
hadn't considered

Is only the canvas upon which life has painted
perpetually changing scenes

                AD2006

The Poet Is Asleep
for Esther Diaz-Martin

The poet is asleep. Yet over the phone I hear your voice
create new worlds (coming into being even now)
Even though I cannot see your face — at the moment
    It is the soul of woman that speaks
She who first
gave the stars   and planets their names

I'm awake   finding
my hands sticky with chocolate

You know awake or asleep it doesn't
matter really   worlds are still
transmitted to me   my lips   find their way
eventually to the breast of a woman

Without idleness   these things would not happen

As brother to Othello the Moor I know for certain

There are but a few words needed
such as "Cebolla morada"
                      "pennant"
                                  or "syzygy"
to move the people to rebellion against the Comprador
You open the door   and I find
myself suddenly the passenger in your car

                          October 16, AD2005

Serenata

Like Munchkins   Earn   after taxes   A swimmer's

Path   It includes   Court Plea for short I, Robot Author

Hang loosely   (Photo)   Serena's sister

Trattoria-tippling

ROAD CURVES

Shangri-Lah   born in bios   Xenia's state

Under siege   Black Sea arm

Roll-Call answer   Galoot

inédits
1. *ix*. AD2007

Horse Dregs On the Road

It's not easy for a horse to step into the milk of spiderwebs. Before a thunderstorm, when all the seasons change and armies are long ensconced in rock, one finds horses' dregs on the road. There is no telephoning from them, nor growth. Anthem-like Maalox in a room of shadows. Interminable worries are suited to an atoll. The fervor of cartoons cannot reach its limpidity.

A castle would implore with its hands but the brown deposits left would continue into offal. As much without knowledge as three pennies which watch a child's unrelieved anger. You ask, "Why this direction?" And then, why not above all things, is it not suited? What else in our time could laugh at the citadel of Tamerlane, without regret or foible? For that matter, what could more respect the *escondido* of my carrying your picture and the moment that I stop that none should see? Or that I should work from an old intolerance toward "a break in the light"? Where I walk toward you, one who did not let his footprints run from him in thunderstorms, as only now the earth does testify. (The earth wants to write its own novel out of horse dregs.)

Throughout the telegraphy of slugs that permeates the silt, the dregs will not let the earth write its novel. Imagine that three patches of horses' dregs could be three countries; they would be left undiscovered until footsteps sloshed the dawn, until a complete "Other" had emerged. Dreams even reluctantly bestow themselves here. Kings come out of a horse's ass. But in coming out, they lose their kingdoms, these names that now all pass into history, like the transposing dates of calendars, or the yawn of volcanoes that never stir. Closed, their coin shops in the afternoon. Let insolence smile as an umbrella.

1974

I Leave The Front Lights On At Night
for B. L. L.

I leave the front house lights on at night, just in case I should miss something in my sleep. I expect that you will vaunt through them stepping outside some intricate murder mystery story, or you will be a lady of the galaxy, sent to give some "coaxing" to the harvest in autumn – always a fabled harvest that you see on the postcards of your childhood. In the meantime, through the luster shining down from the front lights, I hear the mating calls of all the animals of Africa, assembled together in a kind of "parade of progress". You'll come modeling a pink chemise appropriate for a walk through a swamp, or your usual matching blouse and pant skirt. You'll say to me that I've become cynical and perhaps even with the moonlight again try to wipe the irony from my lips as you did once, and as I am an obelisk from Egypt, I'll watch your pain being myself unable to move, as you look with dismay that the irony is the history of Europe on a handkerchief. That is why, my beloved, we should stick to our murder mystery plans. There are so many accessible plots and counter and divers endings to fill in the interim of your coming— when you *do* come, that is. In my sleep I record forever the dream of a woman with a seashell body perched always, wherever I went, on my left arm.

1974

Hommage à Cartier-Bresson
for Will Alexander & Sheila Scott-Wilkinson

So here we are at the Abyss. *L'Abîme, si vous plaît.* Computers have sped up everything. People have to "go away" on "weekends" to make love.

That's immoral. We no longer have the inquiring eye of Cartier-Bresson's Leica camera to tell us that, but we have his *temoignage*, his witness unto.

We should choose to make love whenever we want to and, yes, with whom we want to do so. Of course, between "consenting" adults *(et cetera)*...

But let's face it, even going into the Twentieth-First Century (which Henri Cartier-Bresson glimpsed), "work" has become the shits. I recall when I was a young man, all the pundits of America fretted over what we were to do with so much "leisure" time on our hands once "work" would be carried out by robots and other machines in the Year 2000 A.D. That was, as it happens, some 50 years ago, when these predictions were being made.

Hasn't happened. How many people are there in Asia, Africa or Latin America who choose to work because they love it? How many even choose to so do in the United States, the White Man's bastion of C-I-V-I-L-I-S-A-T-I-O-N?

Cartier-Bresson was, and still is, absolutely right. As others around him were working for the almost 95 years of his life (as he revealed in a TV interview with Charlie Rose), he was "happily having a good time taking pictures, sometimes even painting..." And, no, during this time he didn't live like a king, but one can live grand on cigarettes, French bread, and coffee, I guess, with some cheese and sausage thrown in between. And, of course, French wine was inexpensive back then in the Paris of the Thirties.

But this whole discourse is meant to be of, or on, or about "work", which is getting to be utterly detestable – as are those *compradors* who control the purse strings of those who must work, such that if I speak that word one more time, or even if only utter it in my head, I will strip myself of my clothes and race screaming out the door like Icarus with no Daedalus behind him.

And no *Icarian Sea* to be named after me.

What a monstrous Civilisation we have made (again, I employ this word as my confrère, Aimé Césaire, would, with a sneer) which has invented the word, *work*, or divined its activity! Especially in its modern epiphany. Oh, there was *play* in making pottery perhaps in the 1680's or so. Ploughing the field, a farmer could still look up to the sky and compose a *Georgics.* Oh no, it was never any fun for eunuchs to stand there, fanning their Sovereign and having to stand there, when they couldn't get an erection (although I have never discussed the matter with any *castrati*, nor consulted the memoirs of eunuchs in the T'ang Dynasty).

To work, to make money: the Capitalist has us *by the balls.*

You too, women – especially... The photographs of Henri Cartier-Bresson take us away from the world of work to the inner kingdom of play, of poetry, or what my Friend Léopold Senghor called so aptly *"le royaume d'enfance"*, the realm of childhood, where we are reunited with our true selves, and where we are no longer wage slaves.

The photograph of a man leaping over a puddle – timelessly there, his shadow (sometime *circa* 1934, Paris).

The *voyeur* Cartier-Bresson snapping a photograph of a young man and a girl, both naked, making love. (Henri says he just happened to open the door to to an unknown room and ventured in, not knowing what to expect there. He was surprised – pleasantly so.)

The most important thing Cartier-Bresson has to say about his photographs is that they are just "there", there in *being (l'être)*, and that is the way we must take them, in our being and in the being of himself: "If photography for me ever became 'work' rather than love," to paraphrase his words from the same TV interview, "I would give it up and find something else to do that gave me pleasure. I would maybe play a fiddle! Who knows?"

But, fortunately, that love was maintained and has remained.

A treasure trough of images. A photo gallery of *being*.

They exist as *Snapshots of the Marvellous*, so tenuously taken, as if sneaking up on the Qilin, the fabled chimerical "Chinese unicorn" which can herald good fortune for the one who happens upon the creature.

We know that poetry cannot be defined but these master photographs define poetry for me. If Dylan Thomas could allude to a poetry that for him was "words beyond words", than maybe Cartier-Bresson's photographs foreshadow a way of seeing "images beyond images", a way of being beyond being.

Cartier-Bresson described himself essentially as an "anarchist" in "social-ethical affairs". But he looked to the sky and was continually in awe of its mysteries.

He continued to see through his camera-eye that vastness inside us.

It is perhaps best to end here. The Reader can continue this discourse by opening any album or book privileged to contain the photographs of — — —
Henri Cartier-Bresson.

10-11, August, AD2004

MM Reclining, Reading James Joyce's *Ulysses*

> *douce comme le chant qui etire les yeux*
> ("sweet as the song which stretches
> the eyes") –Saint-John Perse, *Élogues*

Here   beauty   grace and intelligence meet
                    in this one
     "iconic"   moment
                the photo reduced

           to wallet-size   A photocopy of the larger-size
the shot taken by photographer Eve Arnold

  (I don't know if it was "posed")
Or spontaneously
   snapped on the lawn there

It was above all her Spring then
Or it was she who informed the Spring

As the world in its accustomed chaos around her
      encroached   "News"   Of African turmoil
                    Freedom deterred in the deep South
Yet silence maintained its citadel
More enduring than that of Kublai Khan's "pleasure dome"

It was above all her Spring then
Or it was she who informed the Spring

                                March, AD2012

A Faded Pressed Rose Fell From The Pages

Vous qui dormez d'une rose habillée
("You who sleep in a rose dress")
—Georges Schehadé, *Poésies II*

A faded pressed rose fell from the pages
of Rilke's book as I opened it

How long had its fugitive petals hid there?

Perhaps a young woman's fingers
placed it there —
                      for what remembrance?

Why had it revealed itself at this time and place?

What music   contained it once
perhaps conjoined by memories

     of Spain   Africa   France?   What wars or downfalls
encircled its borders   what cries for justice?

Hooves of autumn   storms of summer

I placed the rose there intact again
at the place where someone had written in the margin
"You are the deep innerness of all things"

                                15. *x*. AD2011

On a Leafy Tree-Branch at the Great Wall
for Anna Naruta and Garrett Caples

> *anche le nostre cetre erano appese*
> ("our lyres, too, were hung")
> –Salvatore Quasimodo,
> *Giorno Dopo Giorno*

And indeed here   is its history   shouts of Mongol
invaders across the distant plain
and the delicacy of the pen   of Chinese calligraphy
within its borders   footfalls of a young princess
(now vanished)   espying the "outer world"...

   Here the evolved human thumb culminant
                                      in the violin
of Paganini   My horizon-blue   dress shirt hangs in the closet
    "wrinkle free"   *hecho* in Singapore
The Great Wall photographed in space   visible from
the moon   astronauts circling the earth

could not hear the cry raised by *La Raza* marchers
protesting the death of a young mother-to-be expired
on the fields of the grape harvest —*Uva eorum uva fellis*
—become the grapes of *gall*

The black glove of the Olympian John Wesley Carlos
still leaves its imprint in the air
Rossini's plate of piled-high spaghetti floats by
the halberd of an ancient Han warrior

As neighours at this apartment load their wash
across the way at the complex's laundromat
     unseen behind my door   I wrestle
yet again with the white page

As you both pause   for photos to send home

       — —   sufficient *Sturm Und Drang*   — —

A souvenir Lenin medallion hangs on the tree branch nearby,
floating in the breeze

       "The female of the world overcomes
              the male by stillness" (Lao-Tzu)

Where you stood, Anna, on your visit there as the breeze
blew the silken scarf across your cheek   the moment
of your smile...

                        August AD 2008

D-Day Notes

> *Le ciel de tous les hommes*
> ("The sky of all men")
> – Paul Éluard,
> *Poèmes Politiques*
>
> "The doom of Artreus"
> – Ezra Pound,
> *Pisan Cantos* (LXXVII)

In the dark of D-Day darkness rushing thunderhead clouds
over Gettysburg field
The laundry waits   a paranoia-critical mass
of clothes on the floor
formed in the likeness of a face   floating to shore
Our youth lost there   now come
back to claim it   And hear the whispers
     of Argives in the wooden horse ready to sortie

     There   at the church of *Sainte Mère Église*
   the 82nd Airborne parachutists first to descend   John
Steele's parachute caught there dangling on its spire
remains motionless and frozen   as the strains
of Yanni's music plays "To Live Each Moment To The End"

Depot stops along the way
         Little Rock   and Birmingham
where *pissoirs*   read

"FOR WHITE ONLY"

And   "FOR COLORED ONLY"   (where half of me
       pisses in the water-closet
while the other half whatever-of-me
        pisses in the other)

O whites only amongst the soldiery allowed to dance
with the British girls there in the London nightclub scene
Like John Keats I'm with my boyish face pressed
against the shop window, eyeing the just out of reach "sweets"

In contrast to my lethargies
Mr. Solzhenitsyn works a 14-hour day at his typewriter
(He's now in Vladivostok going across tundra making his way)

Gramsci writes in his *Prison Notebooks*:
    "Every system has its own 'optimum equilibrium'"

   — giving rise to   hegemony —

Enter here   gathering future and past antinomies
a mother's apron   yearbook photos fading one by one
At this hour each of the countenances lost
lining the road "a useless map" of France
                                          Aubade
bird-chirps the troubadours and *trouvères* once heard
"O lover awake! It's time! Hasten before my lord arrives"
On her linen the young man's semen remains   the feel
of his balls clasped between her fingers and palm

        June 6th, 1994, the 50th Anniversary of D-Day

At Oduvai Gorge And the "Beginnings" With "Lucy", The First (Female) Human Being

for Lita and Bear Hornick

...THIS WAY ...CAN YOU HEAR?
Sails of the Argo fluttering in the wind
      in the distance

That's always
"a good sign" — *Why?*
Well, I don't know exactly   Just thought
I'd say that
Now that we're "closer to home"
   (so to speak) have we travelled all
this while without a little *romance?*   I'm thinking

The turquoise Dargha
built by Tamerlane for his wife, Heddy
...Meanwhile
my stomach's
just as empty as that *tombeau*

— —   It would take
the calligraphy of the Han Dynasty
to explain   I loved yesterday

I love Today

And Today's   the moment

      Diane Von Furstenberg goes

QED-TV!

Allez! ¡La Gran Vetreria!
to model her latest
ensemble

    I hereby
        place a pair of golden epaulettes

on the shoulders of naked *Eros* (AKA "Cupid")

Who I must say looks rather silly
flying around there
    in his "birthday suit"!

The latest filibuster

      winds on and on

   it seems endlessly

in the House

"MAH

FELLAH AHMERKANS"

In the year 1865

      "The Negro"

  was *once*

The Republican Vote...

For the "oxymoron" G.O.P. (=*morons, q.v.*)

At the Art Department lecture & slideshow
   on the *Bargello* and the *Ufizzi*

    I find myself in the third row falling
in love once again with Rebecca Albiani, the T. A.,*
along with her ballet slippers

Without *her*

   (And without "Lucy" before her)

There would have been
    no Dante to lead us
in the ways of Love

Nor a Gaudi, nor for that matter

No *Paradiso*   Nor *Tel el-Amarna* style
(Akhenaten's love letters to
    Nefertiti)

 . . . .

Nor Oakies (Tom Joad)   Guelphs or Ghibellines

Nor fires of *Dissent*   to "mix" it all up

And what would the Trade Winds

have made of *that?*

— "LUCY" —

That

    indefatigable *Debutante*

    (Discovered by the Leakeys)

At Olduvai Gorge *dans l'Africa*

    still

Gives us the raspberry!

1992

*T.A., Graduate Teaching Assistant to a Professor.

Ishi the Last Yahi

It has come to this   *Paradise* for me
is a "real" California avocado sandwich (with sprouts
                          and mayonnaise Thank you)
    Thinking
what Buddha said "The true measure of man is
when he learns to walk"
"It takes a man 40 years to learn to walk"

      (Now in my 53rd year on this Planet
        I'm not quite sure I've "learned")

And as I get up at night   it's actually
3 A.M. to practice
my habitual "raiding of the ice box"
                         (as mom used to say)
I begin to pass the cat sitting stoically in the middle of the
living-room carpet at that moment becoming ten times her size
      and illumined as a gigantic sort
of prehistoric sabre-toothed tiger standing
on its hind legs   ready to pounce   However in the next
moment she's back to her "normal size"

meowing as usual   as I go past
At times I admit
I've thought of becoming a "cat psychiatrist"

Outside the door a few blocks away the usual sputter
of semi-automatic weapons
                              (Redwood City in the evening)

air and stars   hanging   above us
a stage curtain

Conclusion: we are not quite
       on the verge
of "civilisation"   as we seem to believe

Old Margaret
          "Keep Your Powder Dry"
                                Mead

Uncle EZ was right   she and the other Anglo
       cabal of cronies
helped to disparage the name of Frobenius
and his discoveries of the WAGADU

And so the anthropologists' frame of mind like that
of the Colonial Imperialists
of this "American Century" of "Speak softly
    and Carry a Big Stick"
sought you out, Ishi, and fawned over you
as a specimen in a bottle
"Cave Man Lives in Museum" *(S.F. Chronicle)*

"Go into a hole in the ground
then they close the door
and go to the sky"

the arrival of the United States as the moral leader
of the White Race...

più nel dolor s'accese ("more in sorrow is lit", from *It.*)

        "Blackjack" Pershing
      (mass murderer of *Wounded Knee)* in France
"Lafayette We Are Here!"

10 A. M. at about this time Maya Angelou will be
at her writing desk with her bottle of sherry
    the hotel room   "without pictures on the wall"

Somewhere the buggers
have preserved ISHI's brain
Ladies who have intelligence in love
    happy I've discovered the Swahili word for
        underwear *nguo za ndani**

                January, 1994

**nguo za ndani,* article of inside clothing

From a Letter to Donald & Luisa Stewart in Rome

> *Aquella hora de crisis... en ese minuto...*
> ("That hour of crisis... at that moment...")
> – Pablo Neruda, *Carta a Miguel Otero Silva,*
> *en Caracas* (1948)

> *Quel est donc ce pays lointain*
> *Qui semble tirer toute sa lumière de ta vie*
> ("What is this distant country/ That seems
> to draw all its light from your life")
> – André Breton, *"On me dit que là-bas..."*,
> *L'Air de l'eau*

There are almond blossoms blowing everywhere

like a snowstorm   and I'm caught in

the midst   like an ancient Chinese poet

who grabs for his pen   to record

the moment   that even in the writing
                      is gone

As I myself will be one day

But the giant images of CHÈ still stand in *Revolutionary Square*

in Havana   and yes "tent cities" (like in the 1930's)
sprung up here   and everywhere
                        in this land

I cannot duplicate the loaves and fishes effected at Galilee

—*Would that I could!*

        As I'm seated on the bench
The mall guard cycling up shouts "How do you like the weather?"
        Ah, it's good   *Muy bien*
    لا بأس! (Mahbsoud! *Ar.*)
    C'est bien, alors
The wind turns the pages
of my notebook

Yet *I breathe*
I breathe the same air Empedocles breathed upon Mt. Etna
Air the Queen of Sheba breathed as she traversed
        many lands on her journey   And we go on
in this air
— ουσία (*Gr.*) — the life of the Universe
continues to flow in us

So a Letter's sent out to Friends   like so many others
in *media res*   mid course
and never quite completed

    Here I pause as I had forgotten
about the Simurgh bird who now takes a little bow
in our little skit washing-machines across the way
in the laundromat still whirring away
at 12.05 A. M. in the apartment complex

Past 3 A. M. in Havana the giant neon image of CHÈ
broods now over Revolution Square

I recall in my dream the lovely young woman
who wrote me a poem

My residence "here"   but a temporary dwelling

It is my *cri*   that goes out

                beyond the nations
  amongst the stars

                      Melina Mercouri
      Lenin   Toussaint l'Ouverture
    Comrade CHÈ Guevara

To renew the face of the Earth

I've found   this fugitive
alcove   along the way
to view the human panorama as it passes by

                March, AD2009

The House Where Karl Marx Lived (Soho, London)

> "A man becomes a fool to engage the prophet's trade"
> – Euripides, *The Phoenician Women*

Here below this window   looking out on the *known*
    universe

Ajax and Hector prepare to do battle before
    their respective camps of the two armies on the field of Troy

Carranza rides his mount ass-backwards   A young woman early
in the morning makes plans   to draw water from the Well of Jacob
in Samaria   Palestine

Below this window   looking out on the *known*
    universe
        Mao Tse Tung sings as he swims across the Yangtze
A whole people swimming with their leader
under starlight
        Then commence the Long March with lit tapers
          to Lushan Pass

beginning as soundlessly   as the Pilgrims' Procession in Berlioz'
    Harold in Italy

A young doctor from Rosario Province, Argentina, looks out
from his book, *The Grundrisse* of Karl Marx

to see the world *awry*   a word in English he will never quite master

(these   events in Space / Time continuum)

And a little boat called *The Granma*
         awaits its moorings
in the Gulf of Mexico   in the choppy currents sets with its crew
to sail to Cuba   where the dates

1282   1789   1776   1917 and the 26th Of July, 1958

meet   where the arrow soars out of Sherwood Forest

Empedocles poised before the volcano crater of Mt. Aetna preferring
to risk the leap into oblivion
         rather than accede to subjugation by the factual world

Shiraz   "City Of The Soul"   Poets Saadi and Hafiz both interred there

         Shiloh Unionists driven back   some of their soldiery
captured in the afternoon   General Buell arrived
"Turn Around Boys" we must face the other way

Vers l'infini   if you will   *Della mia grazia e del mio*
Paradiso   This is said in the midst

Of her tempering smile and the words as yet
unformulated in her eyes
where I strive to be born   *della costellazione che li re risplende*
reaching fulfillment in Kwame Nkrumah

The Marx klan's Sunday picnic baskets taken to the hill on Highgate
Schenectady more or less spelt as it stands *The General Electric*
Company has huge factories and laboratories there
         pastor de strellas   Somewhere, Anya, do you still hear

The reverberations of these words?

надеюсь

союз

большевик *

A dream that falters in daylight   that which
is called "Man" goes
leaf-withered three-footed as a child
I come   again with this sun this Earth   Advance
                              of decadence

Here in the world's great age
    begins anew where I stand   inverted I see
Rodin's *Le Penseur* ("The Thinker")
become the Liberty Bell and yes toilets still flush
in the night as any insomniac will testify
Every member in the series of generations to which I belong
"as a man"   and fleeting   as that designation may be
if we be not altogether of our wits
As the Allenby Bridge making us subject   *were I a swan*

And the power of breathing while we sleep   as to
    "divination"
By dreams the Cumaean Sibyl
sets her leaves before the entrance to her cave   the hour
strikes   for

The Changing of the Guard   held up   his hand

which then flames and burns   but remains

                     A signal-light unscathed beyond

The grid of Mendel   with its tick-tack-toes

Below this window   *looking out on the known*

     universe

where I stand

                     26th Of July, 1995

                        (On the 37th Anniversary of

                           The Cuban Revolution)

* These words: **Надеюсь** (*Russ.*, "Hope")

               союз (*Russ.*, "Union, Soviet")

                        большевик (*Russ.*, "Bolshevik,

                                        Revolutionary")

*   *   *

Gloss to "The House Where Karl Marx Lived (Soho, London)": Verse sections numbered to the Student of the Future, for whatever purposes. As companionate volumes *The Quaderna* by Gramsci, side by side with Dante's *Comedia,* which Marx was known to recite on spontaneous occasions, at picnics at the park with his family. Cited date 1282 refers to *Sicilian Vespers* (refer to the opera of the same name by Verdi), an actual revolution on the Island of Sicily against the French Angevine rulers. Sicily was, and is, the crossroads of the worlds of Africa, Asia and the Mediterranean; the revolt became one of the signal-lights of humanity. The island birth of Persephoné, at Enna, home of the poet's grand parents, the legend recounted to him in his childhood by his grandmother. (Further references, *q.v.*, Milton, *Paradise Lost,* Book IV: 269, of the epic in which Enna is cited.)

Note also: Antonio Gramsci (1891-1937) born in Ales, Isle of Sardinia, philosopher, founder of the Italian Communist Party, himself of Siculo-Albanian ancestry. *Sârd'é* (Phoenician) *It.,* Sardegna. Gramsci, forerunner of "Third World" consciousness, his thought was adopted by the Cuban Revolution as one of the models of Marxist thought and "praxis".

Line 3: Carranza (Venustiano, 1859-1920) President of Mexico. Author of The Constitution of 1917; later counter-revolutionary leader against the great Emiliano Zapata, who can only be ranked in importance to Lenin himself (See Diego Rivera, Rockefeller Center murals, reproduced in the volume, *Portrait of America* by Bertram Wolfe).

Line 16: The Grundrisse: Marx's great Treatise on Political Economy (aka *The Economic Manuscripts) Grundrisse der Kritik der Politischen Ökonomie,* left unfinished in his lifetime.

Line 37: "reaching fulfillment in Kwame Nkrumah" *Presence Africaine* (magazine & publishing house) always in the thrust of the greatest achievements of humankind. Consult pages of Chief Anta Diop (Nations *nègres et culture . . .*) in this instance the culmination of Marx's thought in the First President of the Republic of Ghana (former British colony Gold Coast, Africa); Dr. Nkrumah, graduate of the London School of Economics (U.S. President Kennedy attended as well). Nkrumah's vast visions encapsulated in his *oeuvre, Consciencism: Philosophy and Ideology for De-Colonisation*. Nkrumah, ousted by reactionary forces in Ghana, fought a guerrilla war in the cause of an Marxist-Leninist Liberation of Africa.

For further information on Karl Marx, see also Léopold Sédar Senghor's *Pierre Teilhard de Chardin et la politique africaine* and his *On African Socialism* in English translation. Senghor and Aimé Césaire both associated wth the French Surrealist Group; both were great poets and ideologues of the Third World in the promulgation of *Négritude*. See Senghor's book-length essays *Liberté, tomes 1-5* and *Aimé Césaire, The Collected Poetry*, along with *Solar Throat Slashed: The Unexpurgated 1948 Edition,* by Aimé Césaire, both being bi-textual volumes of Césaire's poems translated in the first instance, by Annette Smith and Clayton Eshleman and then, in the second, by A. James Arnold and Clayton Eshleman.

Epictetus, the Greek and Stoic Philosopher (AD *c*. 55-135), inscribed: "Were I a nightingale, I would act the part of a nightingale; were I a swan, the part of a swan."

Line 57: Allenby Bridge, site of the great treachery, sewing seeds of subsequent Palestinian Arab dispersion and setting Semito-Mediterranean Palestinian Arab Arab against Israeli Settler-Jew. See *Balfour Declaration 1918.*

Line 65: "grid of Mendel" Gregor Johann Mendel (1822-1884) Austrian botanist and priest. Chancellor of the Exchequer of Human Destiny.

Not without a certain awe one wonders how the dawn arrives at 6.21 A.M. with the full chirping of birds. Again, let it be noted that the context of the poem to Marx should squarely inhabit *Shottery,* or the cottage of Anne Hathaway, Village of Warwickshire. This should be considered the womb of all that is English. (And shall I cite the fable of "Should Shakespeare have had a sister?", in my lecture, *A Room of One's Own , by You-Know-Whom*. And what about for background *musik* or Chorus, if you will, to the text "The Home Where Karl Marx Lived", the jingle of the TV commercial "Gimme-A- Break Gimme-A-Break Break-Me-Off-A-Piece-Of-That-Kit-Kat-Bar!")

Line 62: "Changing of the Guard" — At Buckingham Palace. But also, that of the Changing of the Guard at Lenin's Tomb in Red Square in the center of Moscow, implied.

Notice: Not having a word mentioning Paris or The Eiffel Tower has nothing to do with a state of mourning declared over the election of Monsieur Jacques Chirac to the presidency of Whatever Republic. It should be conceded that Paris and The Eiffel Tower are always in the background and implied everywhere between lines written by me. The same Chirac, later on at the end of 2001, upon hearing of Senghor's death (Senghor had lived the last years of his life in Normandy), said, "Poetry has lost one of its masters, Senegal a statesman, Africa a visionary and France a friend". And yet this sentiment did not prompt Chirac, then president of Whatever Republic, or Lionel Jospin, the prime minister, to attend Senghor's funeral in Dakar. It did prompt the scholar Eric Orsenna, writing in the newspaper *Le Monde*, in the wake of France's official failure to attend Senghor's funeral, to entitle his editorial *J'ai Honte* ("I am ashamed").

And thus Marx comes into existence for us not solely in his books but in the efficacy of Lenin's Tomb and the Monument To The Unknown Soviet Soldier: where a young Russian bride still brings her wedding bouquet to be presented there and the sound of the Sea therein reverberates in Red Square. My future wife, wherever you may be, when finally you have taken me into your arms in our first embrace, let us become as the Kalendar Prince and the Young Princess of *The Arabian Nights* once again.

S. T.

The Price of Gold (Again)
On the Market Today at $754.10
for Garrett Caples & for Anna Naruta

It seems to always come in my languor   when I should allow
myself to take a siesta
in the afternoon   A traffic policeman in Athens
    wears a rose in his ear
        (Surely an "earmark" of civilisation   Or
        should we say "near-civilisation"
        as I still believe we haven't as yet arrived there!)

On tonight's NBR
        it isn't Suzanne Pratt who announces it this time
but Suzie Garib (Beauty takes away the acrid taste
    from ill-gotten gain)   Ebony torsos of miners
swathed in sweat
somewhere in Nelson Mandela's homeland

(Etruscan   Minoan   Assyrian   Egyptian) Here I might be found strumming a mandolin or perhaps caressing a mannequin's nakedness

"The on-line world   getting even more crowded"   "*Alors
    avancer transporter esclaves à l'intérieure*"*   On the way
to *Malebolge*   The *Sol   escudos   corazon jaguar   vasija*
— *O royaume!*   My *Hetáiras*
                    passetemps in the ellipse

October AD2007 – August AD2010

Notes:

* *Alors avancer transporter esclaves à l'intérieure* ("Then move to the transportation of slaves from the interior") – Arthur Rimbaud's sojourn in Ethiopia, Oromo region, Abyssinia, about 1888.

Malbolge, c.f., Luogo é in inferno detto Malbolge, Dante, *Inferno,* Canto XVIII:1. "A place in Hell called Malbolge", where panderers, seducers and flatterers were sentenced throughout eternity.

Escudos corazon jaguar vasija, Sp., "shields jaguar heart vessels".

O royaume !, Fr., "O kingdom!"

Hetáiras, Sp., heitaira, also *hetaera,* pl., *hetaerae, Ancient Greek,* were courtesans – educated, sophisticated female companions, not simply prostitutes.

Passetemps, Fr., "pastimes."

The Words "Handle With Care"
(*apparaître tout d' un coup*)
for Harutyun Khachatrian and for Lola Koundakjian

> *ma saison pleine de saisons*
> "my season full of seasons"
> – René Char, *Seuil*

Appear before me out of Nowhere
               which is to say
there is no Nowhere there is Everywhere
Everywhere you have left your shadow
Where you have stepped across the globe
       the instant
of your camera's shutter flicked like a snake's tongue

Sahara's sands
            at your heels
                       Africa's vain glory

The dinner plate left with unfinished food in Aleppo

Your gaze gathered the beauty of women into itself
       perhaps
having seen them only once before you had to move
on to another assignment

At this moment I pause
as I have lost count
sun moon meridian East West all can be captured in New York
reflected in a department store window as one passes by

As I lift my glass of wine in tribute here
to your *converging lens* and the rainbow cascaded there
    on the painter's palette of Arshile Gorky

as I too *partout* meet you
in this Everywhere

                13 April, *Dimanche des Rameaux*, AD2014

L'Origine du monde

for Mlle. Deborah de Robertis

> *Par qui coule en blancheur sibylline
> la femme* ("Through which flows in
> sibylline whiteness the woman")
> –Stéphane Mallarmé, *Don du poemé*

I am awakened by the spent traveller there
lost in the African bush
                          Its lush
presented in a coronal of gold
in the bayou of her thighs

which labour in unforeseen intelligence

in the silence there where ships should embark
for ultima Thule

In the borealis of her
genealogy I cannot trace with origins

in a Cimmerian expanse
laden with offerings

             of holocausts
       and vanished realms

Timbrels of your unbound garment
— O Sybarite
    I recover this
    your history
in my sleep steeped with its dolmens

Dolmens she takes to herself and forms
as if with potter's hands

             October AD2014

Envoy
To Anne Marie Albiach

> *...des prophèts, des sages...que vous avez
> assassiné entre le sanctuaire et l'autel*
> —Matthieu 23. 31-35
> ("...prophets and sages...where ye slew
> between the temple and the altar")
> —Matthew 23. 31-35
> *Douay-Rheims* Version

On *Superbowl Sunday* a banana peel lies spread in the middle of the street. Little men scarcely an inch high with sparks about them emerge out of nowhere to dance about the peel. A man in a baseball hat walks by to the end of the street, then turns and walks back again without even a glance at the banana peel left in the street or the scene taking place in a circle of sparks around the peel.

(We don't know *who* the mysterious Count is)

And is it not possible that all things begin here with this upsurge of dancing one-inch men whirling around in their circle of sparks; and that I am the only one to witness them? – And surely the *Griots* know the significance of this (a tangible sign-if-icance, translatable into the realm of real energy, not the mental constructs of our language aficionados who posit all new non sequiturs for the twilight of the White Man)

Make way! Make way for the poem – do not obstruct it!

I will say it again: the course is between the madhouse and the Abyss ("periit inter altare et aedem" –II Lucam 11.51.) And this is quite simply translated the madhouse being the temple and the altar being the *Abyss* where the prophets were slain at the hands of the hierarchs

Again, admitting to my lifelong fascination with the Bird Woman in trek across the Prairie

البراري

As – Shahadu! Invisibly, Poet, do you now stand beside the family's multi-generational home now being razed by the Occupiers of the land on the *West Bank* (Nablus)?

One of the demolition crew's former European name, Feder, is now Ben-Asher   While eyes of the six-year-old Palestinian child, Bilal, remain fixed on the scene of devastation there... The detonation resounds inside me, on and on, how many years now? I cannot get it out of me

Only then do "things" become tedious *mal* concerns. The man and his pretty wife ogle each other cheek-to-cheek in the mirror (I am given as "The Observer") The strange blue light of evening swaggers outside

26 January AD2003

A Moment in Teheran

Finally!   the world is waking up!   HOORAY!
In the streets of Teheran
While the poet is asleep   thousands of miles away

A giant pen
is writing   FREEDOM   A world ends   A world
begins in the streets of *Teheran*

As a lovely woman screams through the screen of a cell phone
"The system is a <u>fraud</u>!"

Here is the beauty
that has succeeded that of Helen

Here
is the beauty (though her face remains masked to her oppressors)
      of Scheherazade
        &
      of Layla

While I am here   her Majnun*   her muezzin
(At last she has heard my cry)
I see the minarets are dancing   with the sun and moon

Pushkin's *The Bronze Horseman* comes alive
now in a gallop of a thousand legs

There's a red London phone booth flying up in the air

Mon Afrique
Take note:
the stage is set for your next play

In a moment   an eternity
in the streets of Teheran

                                     16 June AD2009

* Majnun: Epic of *Layla and Majnun* by the Persian poet Nizami (13th Cent. A.D.), a prototype for Shakespeare's *Romeo and Juliet.*

Song for Henry Winston (1911-1986)

> *Et je descends dans mon miroir*
> ("And I go down in my mirror")
> – Paul Éluard, "*Mourir*"

It came to me from one of those "senior moments" (as they say)
The memory of when we met for the first and last time
        on the makeshift podium with Dorothy Day
on May Day   50 years ago

        — I remember it like it was yesterday —

Each of us waiting there for our turn to speak
     beneath the fluttering Red Flag with its insignia
of Hammer-and-Sickle   calling for an end of war
        and to feed the poor

As across the way   amongst the jeers and cat-calls
of hate ("Burn the Jews!" "Traitors! Send them all
back to Russia!" "Better dead than Red!")
                they
     brandished their Stars-and-Stripes
alongside the Swastika...

Just then I went "blank"

But to me your blindness said
                and will ever say it all

As Tiresias the Seer journeying through hell

As Schubert's *Wanderer* seeking again
his homeland for refuge which was ever beyond

It remains with me to this day that "homeland" as I pass by
people immobilized in their automobiles
    like those human statues
                      formed out of the clay of Pompeii

                AD2011

A further gloss on Henry Winston: In 1948, having been convicted of revolutionary activity, Winston escaped while on bail. He managed to maintain his activities while underground. Following his surrender to Federal authorities years later, Winston served out his sentence, but was denied medical treatment despite severe health problems. He finally received medical attention in 1960. By then, a tumor had to be removed which left him permanently blind. In 1961, against a backdrop of waves of world-wide protests, the Kennedy administration allowed Winston executive clemency, and he was permitted to seek further medical treatment in Eastern Europe and the Soviet Union.

The Dust of the Pharaohs Flies in the Air
(Tahrir Square, 31 January AD2011)

The dust of the Pharaohs   flies in the air

We have nothing to say   but HOORAY!   And enough
handkerchiefs to protect the nose   This is one
Karl Marx never anticipated   O "optimistic outlooks"!
An abrupt correction   to commentators   This isn't
the Middle East   "Ladies and Gentlemen — IT'S AFRICA!"
       and naturally the Wall Street speculators are "nervous"
(as usual) whenever the voice of the People comes to the fore

And there   the "Moving Finger" writes
Not from the sky but from the streets of "Liberation Square"
TAHRIR   —   —

Whereas here it's an   "assault on salt"

But above the din I hear
the click of women's high heels on
the thoroughfares   of Paris   New York   and   London

as well   from Chippewa Falls
where the always elegant Diane Eastabrook
reports on NBR the latest stock advances of the electric car

                                        31 January AD2011

To the Baghdad School of the Arts

يا بغداد!

O Baghdad!

Recercar   Stephen Hawking   71 years old
(miraculous to have lived so long—
a "terminal illness")   But what has he
told us?   All his calculations and speculation

cannot reach   the heart of the Poem

          Who can measure the line   of movement
between the dancer's toe and her cascading hair?

The statues tell us
Move it! Move it!
          (—Anne Waldman, *Fait accompli*)

Return   to   *Serendip*

Giacometti's workshop   a damp garage

Awake at   6.00 A.M.

And the panoply
   of Woman's Beauty will again be
exposed to me

che la destra del cielo allenta e tira *

that Heaven's right hand slackens
                 and draws taut

12 January AD2012

**che la destra del cielo allenta e tira*, It., "that the right of the sky loosens and pulls"- Dante, *Paradiso*, Canto XV: 6.

The Bridge Across the Nile ("The Arab Spring")
for Mona El-Naggar, Cairo

Nous qui puisons dans l'avenir notre lumière
("We who dip into the future our light")
– Paul Éluard, *"De premier mai en premier mai"*,
Poèmes politiques

The bridge across the Nile   Africa
extends   to all the world
with the words

الهسار !   Tahrir!   نحو الحرية !

—*Al-Hurriya!*

Liberation   Freedom
words that belong
to all men and women   everywhere   of every clime

...*If these were my last words*, these
"words beyond words"*   (*l'Au-delà*)
I hear spoken not only by one but by all.   The *epoch*

of a people from whom the Sphinx sprang
which remains inscrutable   pointing
     to the Absolute   that Absolute   which eluded

                Hegel who proclaimed it
          from his lectern
A cry — *un cri* — that has been repressed for thousands of years

O Friday of Rage   Day of Mahfouz   In this food I eat furtively as a prisoner   in my hands intermingled dust
                           of the Pharaohs

And for you who have inherited the Beauty of Nefertiti, who are her new mirror   in your womanhood

I   with these fugitive words   *salute you*

                          14 February, AD2011

* Dylan Thomas

Manifesto *AU CONTRAIRE!*:
On the Occasion of the Whitney Biennial 2014

To: Michelle Grabner, Professor, School of the Art Institute of Chicago, Zoe Leonard, Artist & Stuart Comer, Chief Curator of DMPA, MOMA

Notary Sojac, as Smokey Stover says,
to unlock the mystery of *existenz*
—1 April AD2014

There are no "Women Artists."

There are no "Men Artists."

There are only Artists

who happen to embody

one gender or another.

When I speak of Art:

I AM ART.

I AM AMONGST THE ARTISTS,

those who are so-called.

Again, *I AM ART.*

That which I do is "Art."

That which I write:

"Everything I do is *poetry.*"

I remain French Surrealist,

and therefore:

Ainsi Mesdames et Messieurs,

Vedi Napoli e muori!

I revive my dictum

after so many years

in abeyance:

"C'est la guerre totale."

TOTAL ASSAULT!

Your museums

and galleries

must open the door

to the Maelstrom

which is US.

A man walking outside in the pouring rain.

Prendre d'assaut! Faire d'orage!

Artists of Colour?

C'est l'Afrique! C'est l'Ethiopie! C'est le Dogon!

There is the veracity of ART,

in the true cradle of Civilisation.

(Not the Tigris or Euphrates, — Sorry!)

It's Africa.

But if you would ask the Question:

"What is Contemporary Art?"

Ask, then, Africa;

ask the Cameroon.

Ask the Siné Saloum!

One must enter

the domain of

the oneiric.

—Thus, my absence

from your midst

is my presence.

ART

what you call "art"

is going on

beyond your conceptions

—*au-delà.*

Beyond the walls

of your galleries

and museums:

Art IS HERE,

where I am.

I speak it each day.

In turn *it* speaks

Ancient Egyptian,

Modern Bambara and Amhara.

It speaks in every word

André Breton ever wrote.

Thus, *AU CONTRAIRE!*

It is inscribed in the journals

of Arshile Gorky;

evidenced also in the paintings

of Gorky

and those

of Jackson Pollock.

It is they

who lead the Maelstrom,

the Siege of the Citadel.

—*Avant! Avant!*

—Yet despite

all philistinism,

Je t'aime.

JE SUIS L'ART.

I am sure *Le Grande Artiste*,

the Cookie Monster,

would agree with me.

Répondre s'il vous plait.

P.S.

My tall next door neighbor's long lovely legs. I am sure

the rocks are happy as she walks on them. *Alors, même*

que je suis encore fatigué. Alas, I am not a Czar

so I can't sweep her off her feet. She knows

nothing about Art. She is one

of the tribe of technophiles,

—*digitalized.*

But there goes Art (in her)

although it knows it not,

—The Unknown,

the Nameless One

(I do not know her name, or station in life)...

but that she goes into a house and

emerges therefrom, —onto

the thoroughfare, past

this window from time

to time.

Now I am all silent.

I recall

that the grand artist

— pope of us all!—

Jackson Pollock

once declared

he would rather cease

talking with human

beings altogether,

in favor of

expressing his *communiqué*

solely in his art of painting.

Bravo! I concur.

Yet I persist

with talk—talk—talk,

when I should *only* write!

And otherwise keep my silence.

"And disguised I sat amongst you.

And you wrapped yourselves

in different webs. Silently,

you guarded

the rusty keys of the gates."

—These words

could have come

from my own mouth

but they did not.

They came from the

Russian artist turned

mystic and pilgrim,

Nicolas Roerich,

who migrated to

the Himalayas to

live his life there.

—For you, who

so tenaciously

guard the rusty keys

to the Gates.

1 April–30 April AD2014

Translations of Foreign Phrases:
Ainsi Mesdames et Messieurs, Vedi Napoli e muori!
("So ladies and gentlemen", *Fr.*, "See Naples and die!", *It.*)
C'est la guerre totale!, Fr. ("This is total war.")
Prendre d'assaut! Faire d'orage!, Fr. ("Assault! Make a storm!")
C'est l'Afrique! C'est l'Ethiopie! C'est le Dogon!, Fr.
("It's Africa! It's Ethiopia! It's the Dogon!")
—*au-delà* (" —beyond") - AU CONTRAIRE!, *Fr.* ("On the contrary!")
Je t'aime. JE SUIS L'ART, Fr. (" I love you. I AM ART.")
Répondre s'il vous plaît, Fr. ("Please respond")
Alors, même que je suis encore fatigué, Fr.
("Then, even if I am still tired.")

In This Resurgence:
On Reading *"Collected Poems, Joseph Ceravolo"*

>*Sin arrimo y con arrimo*
>("With and without a mainstay")
>–San Juan de la Cruz, *Glosa*

With this resurgence "in the world's heart
I leave this heart murmuring..."
    — Friend! Soul Brother now in the vastness of the Holographic
      Universe overseeing
I underline and *exégèse*
these lines in your tome

To make of them further words for *mèmoire*
culled from my Communist comrades' *Mundo*
but there's room enough for clouds, too
and an ashough's *Song For Woman*

I remain
Love-crazed taken
completely by surprise within this refuge

Hafiz's 'Tavern of Ruin'*   and continued
the absurdity of the world outside *(you knew so well)*

Dresden "mourning march"
                              its anti-fascist blockade
                                                    13 February, 2010
                    succeeded
          no doomsday scenario
                    was recorded

   Yet here in Eudora Welty-Land   the magnolia
trees still call out the moans of lynched Black men there
The Argo's sail in disrepair
—so unexpected

                              4 October, AD2013

* "Do not enter the 'Tavern of Ruin' / without observing its manners /
for the dwellers at the door / are the confidants of the King"
—Hafiz, 14th century Persian poet.

Actuelles of Dr. Pangloss,
or An Omphalic Note for "*Terre de diamant*"
for Nanos Valaoritis & Marie Wilson-Valaoritis

> *Et toi, le sang des astres coule en toi*
> ("And you, the blood of the stars
>   flowing in you")
>   – Paul Éluard, *"Une"*,
>   *Capitale de la douleur*

The trails of Discoverers of the New World
have long been obliterated

At the moment I discern this, there is just so much
macaroni and cheese left in the pot

Friends, my hands ever confer
their blessings upon you both as hundredfold
hands of the Sun-god Ra upon the pharaonic couple
Nefertiti and Akhenaten of Luxor
(the illumination comes through me yet I have no
knowledge how it's done, or the origin of its source of light)

My Kateri Tekakwitha
                Lily of the Mohawks
                              concenters

in her breast the quantum which gathers there and diffuses
here in these rosebuds   enclosed
in the folds of a love letter
the sanctifying process of evolution
                                        from amoeba Thesis
and Antithesis seahorse foetus
                                        to Man-and-Womankind
a footnote to Empedocles and the Dogon cosmologies

As once again opening in the timeless realms of the empyrean
RAF Spitfire pilots spectrally step forth onto
a carpet of cloud   rendering unto us their open-hand salute

                      *   *   *

We are a long way from Missolonghi, friends
Hello Dino   (Siotis)
Hello Gianni   (Chioles)
Hello Thanassis   (Maskaleris)

                                        Γειά σου   Encore!

But the fumes thereof of the gunpowder is still there. I could smell it
in the Café Mediterranean (Berkeley, CA) where we used to meet.
(I have still the lovely letter sent to me by Mrs. Kazantzakis at that
time, taking the U. S. to task for the betrayal of Cyprus in favour of
the Turk occupier.)

It's a Wednesday. My pen's clogged. I have just witnessed a book of wonders, photographs of one of the loveliest women in the world, who could have truly become a surrealist woman, but who is now relocated, from this life in Space/Time beyond our dimension (*circa* 1994).

But, Nanos, it is to you who have there with you *the* Surrealist Woman known to us as MARIE WILSON. I still recall the weekend excursions of my wife and myself to your house in Oakland and that photograph by Embirikos of you both in the bloom of an epithalamium.

The "red flags" wave on. When you want to write a book, the sphinxes' demolitions return the bitter taste of the Bosporus. I have just awakened, having had too much *Metaxa*, dreaming again that I was shipwrecked on a remote Greek island in the Aegean, but I actually have woken up on the seaside beach at the poet Morton Marcus's house in Santa Cruz, CA (*circa* 1969).

*   *   *

As regards Surrealism, it continues to be my perspective. The photograph of you, Marie and my old departed friend Ted Joans is gone also. But we remain despite geography, rainstorms, beginnings and endings, gains and losses.

I am notified right at this moment that one of the floorboards in Walt Whitman's house in Camden (NJ) has sprouted Koranic angel's wings to join in with us.

As I scratch my beard, a door closes next door. I'm reminded we haven't as yet exited the mystery of Gravity — thus the heroism of Daedalus in inventing flight as he studied birds soaring above the earth of his confinement. Secrets of Time and Space contained in the mirror as I turn once again the pages — spectral pages to be sure — of the *Terre de diamant*. I am rejoined to myself. I hear the celestial song of the *Seeress Diotima* as she expounds upon the transcendence of Love.

Xaipe!

(as I hold my pen its petals close   like
a flower at night)

Salute à nous de le Septième Ciel! (Salute to we of the Seventh Heaven!)

Salute à nous de le Huitième Mer! (Salute to we of the Eighth Sea!)

12 June –13 June, AD2014

Note: Γειά σου, *Gr., Hello; Xaipe, Gr., Rejoice*

Témoignage à Senghor
To Léopold Sédar Senghor

—*Dakar le 9e Avril, 1969*:

"bien reçu votre letter ...qui m'a beaucoup emu.
  Bien sûr, j'ai subi l'influence du *Surréalisme*, mais à la verité, ...très peu, car *le nègre est par nature, Surréaliste*"
  – Letter from the Poet, Léopold Sédar Senghor,
  To the Author, S. T.

["received your letter, was much moved by it... To be sure, I have acknowledged the influence of Surrealism upon me, but only to the extent that the person of Black Ancestry is (in himself already) innately Surrealist."]
  –Translation from the French by the Author, S. T.

"Une proposition qui émane de moi — — ...
— — que tout, au monde, existe pour aboutir à un livre"
  – Stephane Mallarmé, *"Le Livre, instrument spirituel"*
  From *Quant au livre* ("As for the Book")

"(I can say) a proposition which has emanated from myself (to the effect) that *everything* in the world exists to *culminate in a book*"
  –Translation from the French by the Author, S. T.

3e mars AD2003

     I am greedy even with the last moments of daylight at dusk. Had your name not been disclosed to me I should have known what it means to live in a world without hope *(L'Espoir)*   Without the light from your torch my *pérégrinage,* my journey, — my *Hadj* — would never have been impeded by some 200 or more years   I have never really learned to

                                                                   play cards (all my earliest attempts at games were the butt of jokes by my puerile companions who would have been called by the Plains Indians of the American West "white-eyes", and also by the phrase of my grandmother which I recalled from my boyhood referring to that race amongst whom we had settled that prided itself on its superiority, those whom she called "ghost-faces")

     "It is easier for a camel to go through the eye of a needle"   I do not know why that Saying comes to mind but as it does I feel you would be its best interpreter as you had stored within yourself so many of the world's follies as to outdo even the sage Democritus in "search for but one honest man"

     You who presented me with the *African Prince*

     Who *divined* the French Language   gave it its *inimitable*ness of song as spoken by an African tongue (as opposed to that nasal *choucrouterie* as spoken by modern "Parisians")

     — — *Now*   in this barren hour   when I have my hands held up to me as mirrors exposing the pink of my palms and outstretched to the horizon - they - these hands reveal only a ravaged harvest the wordless *De Profundis* of a Verdun battlefield still smouldering *(such is the vision of the world)*

Out of "airy nothing"
                                A giant Dogon mask of the harvest-season
yields its telluric word   The *Nomo* of the cosmos

    As the Angel with the burning coal upon the lips of the prophet

    I am given the *gift of speech* once again
    Ecce tetigit hoc labia tua... Ecce ego, mitte me
    ("*See, this has touched your lips... Here am I, send me*")

    Above the soundless twaddle of men of the marketplace

    Above the buyers and sellers of gold and men and women's souls (Those who signed the Constitutions of Laws and affixed their signatures to the Bills of Sale of Slaves, who set a price for the *Wolof* mother and daughter upon the Auction Blocks of Europe and the
                      "Slave Market" at Louisville Georgia)

…Now before me appear those fading footprints of women I once loved; since left for all corners of the Earth

       Paris   Beirut   Dakar   São Paulo
) (O São Caétano do Sud!

    Now the young woman voted off the *Survivor* "Reality" TV
        show speaks as the augury for our time
                "That's the way it is in
                this game."

Ronsard's *spectre* repines as to what "is" and "what is not suitable" for poetry.

    Then I ask: "And what would *The Pleiades* have seen in my old friend Rauschenberg's "White Paintings"?

But here we recognize the essentially Eleatic lines

Une brise passé dans le nuit

("A breeze passes in the night"
–Teilhard, *Le Mélieu Divin)*

* * * *   * * * *

8.26 A.M. They put on their hats and coats and head out the door. Everywhere (this scene is enacted).

To work. "Going to work."

While I rise to face the desert of the *Unknown*.
Hoping therein I might find the oasis of *The Poem*.

Simón del desierto   *Simeon Stylites*   spent 40 years in retreat from the world on top of an ancient pillar in the desert. How did he keep from going *mad?* (One never knows if he succeeded in avoiding ultimate madness in his *askesis*.)

The practice of his meditation and prayer, sun-up to sun-down and sometimes through the night, no sleep at all.

A look at the page: "Will these be the only words today?
Will these be the last words, *les derniers mots?*"

I envy those who so easily or routinely put on their hats and coats and "head out the door."

* * * *   * * * *

Le Quotidien! The *Quotidian*, "from which
a thousand winged Pegasuses take flight each day"

The pocket-sized photo   found on the street
with its frame of shattered glass   a studio portrait
of two Black children   (sisters)   Were their own ancestors

As yours (Senghor)   Of the *Mandingues* in the Disapora

Of the "New World"   —*En l'Amérique d'aujourd'hui*
In all likelihood
these schoolchildren have never heard
                          of the name of Léopold
           Sédar Senghor
Or that of Peré Teilhard de Chardin
                These sisters whose
         Smiles reach now toward   the Unknown
                                  I realize, then
I do not know if the two portrayed in this frame
         are living or dead

Fanfares of   Victor Hugo's *Jean Valjean*
"Prisoner No. 24601" reach out to them

Yet our bloodlines meet in the tributaries
of the Siné-Saloum

And culminates in the Corinthian column's *acanthus*

xxxxxxxxxxxxxxx

A horse whinnies and continues its gallop in my bed

As I rise   As *Pélerin*
And no doubt a couple still dances next-door to the "Big Band
sound of the '40s Glen Miller   (that" next-door
being removed from Time and Space)   where I remain
here but one of the roses from   Sa'adi's *Gulistan*
(and even this along with the others has turned to ash)
As the clothes-closet mirror (again) accuses me of
                                        thievery
_ ****   ****   ****   **** _

   (Photo of Senghor and *Consort*, The *Princess de Hauteville*)

All that would be of her then

That *haut* brow   Where mysterious songs of *La Bretagne* accede the
emerald against the ivory bodice birds of dawn
(The *Pélerin*   reflects there as he holds   bridle of the horizon)
       "– Where once the beauty of ancient queens was
spoken of" I give out the website address *www.barbarasher.com*, again,
myself having no computer, to the girl who might pursue her own
dreams (but never knowing the outcome
                              of the same) *Il est bon et just*   It is
mete and right at this time
For the *Noumenal* realm (as the *thing-in-itself*) as the swirled chambered
nautilus journeys and I myself never come closer"

On the approach that of a Tuareg's veil   orisons there
in harshness of the winds   prospects   Her high-heels hidden in
                       the gown's wake   Challenge then
not of succumbing the while recognizing victory's habitation in
the house of submission   that tendril of the *vas deferens*
      Where moons are born
      All that would be of her then
Of this very Summer
      Morning   (She doesn't know)
I go invisibly to reap the song in the loggia
                            of her hair
As she spoke to me, saying
         "My husband and I   go to *video*
    on weekends"   (As it would have
been in *Gatsby's* time. The couple filmed social
                            events)

        I have struggled
with a bit of cumin seed
caught between my teeth
throughout the night. To find the right *timbre*
The French I inscribed in her book
(She never asked for its translation)

        The mystery of *Motion*   its   *élan*
The motion of rising from one's bed   *(the caress*
that remains on the cheek long after
the partner has gone to work)   Motion of workers
who built the *pyramids*   waves   of their
countless minions   the nameless builders gone

(As *motion*   continues long after
                    the action   completed /
Mozart's pianoforté facing the unknown
now sits silent in the room in Vienna)

                              Asserting that it was
"we" *(Nous)* who invented the *soul*, Mallarmé was in error in this

       (But is these spaces   let them read the histories of
those kings and queens whose course was set not upon conquest
                                        but upon seeing into the
secrets of the Universe   and dissolving of the self in the act of giving)

— Revealed   in the aurora borealis   of insomnia —

Then, *Africa,* are you confirmed in placing
your prophet's mantle over the bare-shoulders
of *Man-And-Woman-Kind*

"*The decisive step* taken: *the human hand*
Become *free* to attain ever newer skills
Thus the hand not only the organ of *labour* but also
the product *of* labour... has enabled it to conjure into
being the painting of Raphael, the music of Paganini
(Homo Faber)
With Man we enter History."
(— Engels

..."Out of the aridity of desert sands a splendid flower
a vase of Venetian glass" (Out of that land the European
said had "no history" *History* was born

    Not of Adam but of *LUCY Of Olduvai Gorge*)

  ...As you disclosed *Africa* remains the key (For Man-And-Woman-Kind)

Thus "my tongue is the pen of a ready writer"

The *Noösphere*   Which defines my pilgrimage

                                    —à l'Horizon

To the door of the *horizon*

C' EST *formidable!*

Salut à le Van Gogh de notre temps

(For The Van Gogh of our era)

S. T.

Juillet AD 2011.

From My Granddaughter, MAYA: (4yrs old)

"Grandpa's House"

*From Maya
to
Grandpa-
"House"
-8 Dec. AD2006*

Maya Torregian-Gustaveson, 8 December, AD2006.

www.ingramcontent.com/pod-product-compliance
Lightning Source LLC
Chambersburg PA
CBHW080341170426
43194CB00014B/2640